Saint Francis

and the Way of Lent

Other volumes for this series:

Saint Francis

and the Way of Lent

Primary Sources from
Francis of Assisi: Early Documents
for Devotional Use

Jon M. Sweeney

series editor

Francis of Assisi Spiritual Practices series

New City Press
Hyde Park, New York

Published by New City Press
202 Comforter Blvd.,
Hyde Park, NY 12538
www.newcitypress.com

Library of Congress Control Number: 2021921978

ISBN: 978-1-56548-712-3 (paper)
ISBN: 978-1-56548-713-0 (e-book)

Printed in the United States of America

Contents

General Introduction

The *Francis of Assisi Spiritual Practices* series utilizes the texts and translations of New City's groundbreaking and now complete *Francis of Assisi: Early Documents, Volumes 1-4* (1999-2020) to offer readers of all backgrounds inspiring, encouraging, and challenging entry-points to the essential issues of a Christian life in the twenty-first century. Each book in the series should appeal particularly to readers who desire to walk the Way of Saint Francis with relevance to his life, writings, and legacy. We created the series with the conviction that the Way of Francis is as relevant today as it was eight hundred years ago.

The first four volumes have been planned. The one you are holding, *Saint Francis and the Way of Lent*, is the first. Coming soon are these three:

- *Saint Francis and the Problem of Possessions*

- *Saint Francis and How We Relate to Fellow Creatures*

and

- *Saint Francis and the Big, Wide, Lay-led Church*

Each will be presented in a four-week format and designed for both individual and group use. Each week, or chapter, focuses the reader on a theme that is central to that volume's overall theme. Short introductions are written by the editor and designed to preface selections from the primary texts from the *Francis of Assisi: Early Documents* volumes, and these are each followed by questions for discussion or reflection. There are six readings for each week, followed by final prayers of intention and spiritual practice suggestions for that week on that theme.

We would love to hear from you, as to how you are using these books, and how to improve them for future editions. Also, our hope is to continue this series with additional titles, as demand and time and God permits. Your feedback will be an important step along the way for us to do that well. Please write to us at newseries@ newcitypress.com. *Pace e bene.*

Jon M. Sweeney
Series Editor
June 13, 2021
The Feast of St. Anthony of Padua

Introduction to This Volume

We often downplay penance today. Self-care has been the ascendant idea, even in Christian spirituality, for at least a couple decades. As a result, penance has often been turned into a stereotype and is easily regarded as an anachronism. For example, there is no better way to signal the deep-set evil of a movie character than to show him flogging himself alone in his basement, a crucifix hanging on the wall in front of him. That's how we have sidelined penance, too, as if it is "medieval," irrelevant, and all about self-inflicted pain.

It is also a stereotype when penance during Lent is reduced to such sacrificial acts as giving up chocolate or movies for a brief time. When this is the extent of our use of penance, we have lost the sense of sacrifice that it is meant to contain.

"Preaching penance" is what Francis of Assisi began to do from the earliest moments of his conversion, and when he sent his brothers out into the world he instructed them to do the same. By this he meant much more than our little givings-up for Lent each year.

Even more subtly, it has become unpopular even to talk about penance. Penance is what many people feel we no longer need. Nor guilt. Nor, in some quarters, sin. These have become common theological and therapeutic assumptions. We are supposed to correct the mistakes of the past by taking better care of ourselves, not by beating ourselves up, which is how those Hollywood portrayals have led us to understand penance. God intends us to be happy, and happy people are supposed to "be good to themselves," rather than waste their time on the mistakes of the past or by becoming paralyzed with guilt.

Pope Francis, after all, has emphasized mercy more than any other quality of God. God is mercy, and we are to be a merciful people. We add a resounding Amen to this.

But God also intended us to recognize some mistakes, faults, and vices not simply as mistakes, but as sins. Pope Francis has preached and taught a lot on this subject, as well. And sin can take on a power and influence in a human life that can't and shouldn't be ignored and should be taken seriously. The best remedy for many sins is to try to root them from our lives through penance properly understood and regularly practiced.

Francis of Assisi—our lovable saint who talks with animals and dances when he preaches—took sin, penance, and conversion very seriously. Personal sin (in individual human lives) and corporate sin (for which we are all responsible) are addressed again and again in his writings and in the accounts of his life. This attention to sin and penance can make some people today feel uncomfortable. That's okay. It *should* make us feel uncomfortable. We easily accommodate and excuse sin; Francis of Assisi won't allow us to do that.

(In his own life he also sometimes went overboard in his personal enthusiasm for penance, and we won't overlook those mistakes here. We'll talk about that, too.)

Penance is about conversion, and conversion is the work of a lifetime; it involves a change of heart. In the gospels, Jesus preaches to his followers using the Greek word, *metanoia*, which means both "penitence" and "change of heart." Sometimes the word is used as a verb, meaning to "do penance," and this is always for the purpose of discovering the "change of heart" that is like a conversion. The interior work and the exterior work are intrinsically linked.

This is true in Francis's writings and life as well. For example, see how he began his "Testament"—one of his final writings, and certainly his most autobiographical. These are the opening sentences:

> The Lord gave me, Brother Francis, thus to begin doing penance in this way: for when I was in sin, it seemed too bitter for me to see lepers. And the Lord Himself led me among them and I showed mercy to them. And when I left them, what had seemed bitter to me was turned into sweetness of soul and body.[1]

More than anything else, we can begin to understand Saint Francis—and Jesus, while we're at it—in the context of penance and Lent as a way of life. We need to accept that we are sinful, that we sin with regularity, and that each sin is meaningful. The sin in our lives needs to be addressed.

---

1. *Francis of Assisi: Early Documents (The Saint)*, 124. In every case, we reproduce the texts as they appear in the *Early Documents* volumes, except that, where it exists in the original series, we remove the verse-numbering of passages.

What we are to do, we hear most beautifully in the Bible through the words of the prophet Joel:

> Yet even now, says the LORD, return to me with all your heart,
> with fasting, with weeping, and with mourning;
> rend your hearts
> and not your clothing.
>
> Return to the LORD, your God, for he is gracious and merciful,
> slow to anger, and abounding in steadfast love,
> and relents from punishing. (Joel 2:12-13)

We are on this earthly journey to prepare ourselves for heaven, and our conversion journey is all about changing our hearts.

Week One

Lent as a Balanced Way of Life

This is where we start in the first book in a new series that aims to present short selections from the writings of and about Francis of Assisi on essential topics for living a Christian life. Lent and Lenten practice were important to Francis, as can be seen in the stories from his life and in his own writings.

And every Christian life should pivot around Lent.

The Rule of St. Benedict declared: "The life of a monk ought to be a continuous Lent."[2] Francis was not a monk—he was a friar—but he agreed wholeheartedly with this classic monastic statement and fashioned his life around this principle. Not only did he observe the traditional Lent that occurs each year leading up to Easter, but he observed multiple Lents, and Lenten practices, throughout the year.

Conversion does not take place all at once. It is a process, one that is life-long, and then some. This is why, in Thomas of Celano's foundational original biography, *The Life of Saint Francis* (which we will quote often), you will see Thomas frequently framing the chronology of

---

2.   *The Rule of Saint Benedict in English*, ed. Timothy Fry, OSB (New York: Vintage Books, 1998), chapter 49:1; 49.

what happened with words such as "in the third year of his conversion. . .", or "in the sixth year of his conversion. . .", or "in the thirteenth year of his conversion. . .".

For this first week, our focus will be set on how and why Lent and Lenten practice is a way of balancing all the responsibilities we have as adults living in the world. Basically, we need what Lent gives us. Lent is a gift. Lent and Lenten practice have a way of sorting all the other aspects of our lives—from responsibility and work to feasting and hallelujahs. And when Lent involves penance, we need to realize that penance is not punishment. Penance is a gift.

What we're aiming at with our penance is conversion of the heart—we want our hearts to be made for God. That's not meant to be a metaphor. Remember the passage from the prophet Joel referred to above. We usually do this in Lenten practice by what the Catechism of the Catholic Church calls "Interior Penance," saying: "Jesus' call to conversion and penance, like that of the prophets before him, does not aim first at outward works, 'sackcloth and ashes,' fasting and mortification, but at the *conversion of the heart, interior conversion*" (#1430).

Francis emphasized that this is the work or a lifetime, and it was meant to be interior work that friars would incorporate into their lives throughout the year, not only or simply during the liturgical season of Lent.

Reading 1

Let's begin with an excellent early summary of Franciscan values and responsibilities: the daily ways that those on the Way of Francis will exercise their vocation in the world. This is a chapter from *A Book of the Praises of Saint Francis* by Bernard of Besse, a friar writing in the years immediately after the death of Bonaventure.

Bernard surveys the conversion and ministries of Francis through the lens of "Employment," meaning, work, or the range of responsibilities that Francis's vocation entailed. Bernard also summarizes Francis's concern that each person who desires to live a life committed to Franciscan values should be employed in similar ways.

A Book of the Praises of Saint Francis
Bernard of Besse

Chapter 6
Employment[3]

The holy man [Francis] always insisted on progress in doing good, remembering that the lukewarm, who do not apply themselves constantly to some work, would be quickly vomited out of the Lord's mouth. No idler could appear in his presence without feeling the sharp bite of

---

3. *Early Documents: Vol. 3 (The Prophet)*, 49-52.

his criticism. He wished his brothers to apply themselves always to prayer or to some good work.

He rejoiced upon hearing that the brothers in a hermitage in Spain had so divided their time, that one part of the week was dedicated to care of household chores, and the other to contemplation. There, one day, when one of those contemplating did not come to table, he was found in his cell lying on his face on the ground, stretched out in the form of a cross, and showing no signs of life; not a breath or a motion. At his head and at his feet there flamed twin candelabra, which lit up the cell with a wonderful golden light. After the light unexpectedly disappeared, he was left in peace; the brother returned to his human self, immediately came to the table, and confessed his fault for being late.

The saint used to speak against the disease of *acedia*: "When a servant of God gets disturbed about something, as often happens, he must get up at once to pray and remain before the most High Father until he gives back to him the joy of his salvation."

He was occupied as the occasion demanded with preaching and with the salvation of his neighbors. How much he accomplished in teaching and the people's conversion is known to God alone, who opened the Scriptures to him so that he could understand and teach them.

A cardinal, questioning him about some obscurities, said: "I'm not asking you as a scholar, but as a person who has the Spirit of God, and so I gladly accept the meaning in your answer, because I know it comes from God alone."

When asked about the words of Ezekiel: If you do not warn the wicked man about his wickedness, I will hold you responsible for his soul, whether we are bound to warn each one whom we know to be in mortal sin, he said: "If that passage is supposed to be understood in a universal sense, then I understand it to mean that a servant of God should be burning with life and holiness so brightly, that by the light of example and the tongue of his conduct, he will rebuke all the wicked. In that way, the brightness of his life and the fragrance of his reputation will proclaim their wickedness to all of them."

He taught not only by example, but also by word strengthened by the miraculous signs which you will find in his life. I refer to what is known to have happened at Alessandria in Lombardy. He was invited by a God-fearing man and asked to eat of everything set before him, in observance of the holy gospel. A piece of capon was placed on the table just as a man was at the door fraudulently seeking help for God's sake. Once he heard the Lord's name, the saint gave him a piece of capon on some bread. The wretch kept it and while the saint was preaching the next day, he shouted to the people: "This is what this Francis is like, whom you honor as a saint. Look at this meat that he gave me last night when he was eating." Then what he maintained was a piece of capon was seen to be fish so everyone chided him. At last that wretched man, dumbfounded by the miracle, was forced to confess what the others acknowledged, and, before every- one, he asked the saint's pardon, admitting his bad will. The meat returned to its own kind, after the liar returned to his right mind.

The saint was brilliant with great power in expelling demons and the grace of healing. For his deeds were especially in the power of the cross. Through the sign of the cross he gave sight to the blind, cast out demons, and healed various illnesses. At Orte someone had a tumor the size of a large loaf of bread between his shoulders. When he was blessed by him, he was instantly so fully cured that not a trace of his tumor remained.

The fervent devotion of people very often offered bread and other food for him to bless. These they kept for a long time, preserved from spoiling by divine gift; when they were eaten bodily illnesses were healed. It has even been proven that such foods had the power to ward off violent thunderstorms and hailstorms. Many claim that through the cord that he wore and patches from his clothes, illnesses were, in the same way, put to flight, fevers ceased, and long-sought health returned.

Once he accepted the hospitality of a knight whose only son had drowned. The youth's body had been sought for a long time but never found. He was distressed at the weeping of the mourners at the boy's funeral. But now the time was at hand when Christ would show forth His wonders in confirmation of the true faith that the holy man was preaching to those who, customarily, poured out their pious and devout prayers to him. By pointing out the spot where he was entangled in the river by his clothes, and, after calling upon Him Who raises the dead, by miraculously bringing him back to life, he then freed his home from a double sorrow. Behold the faithful servant imitated his merciful Lord who, moved by mercy, raised from the dead the only son of a widowed mother! Behold another Elijah and Elisha who, we read, raised the sons of their hosts!

Even irrational creatures obeyed him. For example, one time when the croaking of frogs in a lake near a church interrupted his preaching, he told them to be quiet, so that he too could give praise to God. They were silent after this, until later at another time he re- turned to the same church. When he was told that they were always silent after his word, sorry for delaying them for so long a time, he commanded them to praise their Creator as usual. Old-timers in talking about these two events, that is the events of the frogs and the boy raised from the dead, testified that they saw them. One of them, called Brother Veritas [Truth], said that his tomb is famous for miracles.

Insensible things also seemed to obey. Once, after a general chapter was celebrated at Assisi, Brother Monaldo and about thirty other brothers remained to speak to blessed Francis about the salvation of the soul. He ordered that a meal be given to them since they wanted to leave the next day. Since the procurator had only a small amount of bread, the poor Francis sent word to Clare so that, if she had any, she would send some bread to him for breakfast. At that time, she had only three loaves of bread and sent two. He placed these, divided into small pieces, on the table together with the other small amount, saying: "This is the bread of charity." What more? From these three loaves, those brothers had their fill and from what was left over a full basket was taken away.

There are many signs that neither memory nor any writing retain through which Christ distinguished His herald and sign-bearer, Francis, distinguishing his teaching with a truly undeniable certitude. When we come to work in teaching and other activities, however, we do not shun idleness, which is the death of the soul. Let us be taught by the example of the father, and certainly of Christ Himself, Who was poor and in labors from youth.

I read about a certain brother who said fifty psalms each day that the Lord would guard him from the pains of purgatory. One night, when he was spending the night in prayer, the Savior together with the Blessed Virgin appeared to him and, on Christ's right side, was a large cross touching heaven. The Lord said to him while he was praying: "Work confidently and do penance, for, while I was in the world, I always labored." Let us, therefore, follow Christ and Saint Francis in labor, that we may be joined to them in rest. The industrious Lord does not love a lazy servant.

Reflect or Discuss

1. In the second paragraph, the account of the friars living in Spain, why do you think Francis singled out for praise the way they divided their time? Why is that important?

2. What are some of the different ways that Francis worked, according to this summary account?

3. How does Francis's industry and value of work cause you to rethink what you've always heard about the "Protestant work ethic"?

4. What does the author say about idleness? About Christ and work?

5. What do you think about that last line? "The industrious Lord does not love a lazy servant."

Reading 2

This is another place to begin to discern the Way of
Francis, and to see how it is distinctively Lenten: we turn
to Francis's own writings.

If Lent is a balanced way of life, then the values
and activities of Lent are meant to inform every week
and month and season of our lives. In this last version of
the First Order Franciscan Rule written during Francis's
lifetime, two of the chapters speak to the saint's instructions on prayer, fasting, and other teachings regarding
the penances of a life that's Lenten.

The Later Rule (1223)

Francis of Assisi

Chapter 3
*The Divine Office, Fasting and How the Brothers Should
Go About in the World*[4]

Let the clerical [brothers] recite the Divine Office
according to the rite of the holy Roman Church except-
ing the psalter, for which reason they may have brevia-
ries. The lay [brothers], however, may say twenty-four
Our Fathers for Matins, and five for Lauds; seven for
each of the Hours of Prime, Terce, Sext, and None,
twelve for Vespers, and seven for Compline. Let them

---

4.   *Early Documents: Vol. 1 (The Saint)*, 101-02.

pray for the dead. Let them fast from the feast of All Saints until the Lord's Nativity. May those be blessed by the Lord who fast voluntarily during that holy Lent that begins at the Epiphany and lasts during the forty days which our Lord consecrated by His own fast; but those who do not wish to keep it will not be obliged. Let them fast, however, during the other [Lent] until the Lord's Resurrection. At other times they may not be bound to fast except on Fridays. During a time of obvious need, however, the brothers may not be bound by corporal fast. I counsel, admonish and exhort my brothers in the Lord Jesus Christ not to quarrel or argue or judge others when they go about in the world; but let them be meek, peaceful, modest, gentle, and humble, speaking courteously to everyone, as is becoming. They should not ride horseback unless they are compelled by an obvious need or an infirmity. Into whatever house they enter, let them first say: "Peace be to this house!" According to the holy Gospel, let them eat whatever food is set before them.

Chapter 6
Let the Brothers Not Make Anything Their Own;
Begging Alms, the Sick Brothers[5]

Let the brothers not make anything their own, neither house, nor place, nor anything at all. As pilgrims and strangers in this world, serving the Lord in poverty and humility, let them go seeking alms with confidence, and they should not be ashamed because, for our sakes,

---

5.   *Early Documents: Vol. 1 (The Saint)*, 103.

our Lord made Himself poor in this world. This is that sublime height of most exalted poverty which has made you, my most beloved brothers, heirs and kings of the Kingdom of Heaven, poor in temporal things but exalted in virtue. Let this be your portion which leads into the land of the living. Giving yourselves totally to this, beloved brothers, never seek anything else under heaven for the name of our Lord Jesus Christ.

Wherever the brothers may be and meet one another, let them show that they are members of the same family. Let each one confidently make known his need to the other, for if a mother loves and cares for her son according to the flesh, how much more diligently must someone love and care for his brother according to the Spirit! When any brother falls sick, the other brothers must serve him as they would wish to be served themselves.

Reflect or Discuss

1. In the first selection, note the various "Lents" that Francis identifies specifically. He mentions three. How do these correspond to the calendar?

2. Why so many Lents?

3. Can you think of ways that chapter 6 epitomizes a Franciscan life as a distinctly *Lenten* form of Christian living?

4. Notice how chapter 6 emphasizes the friars are "pilgrims and strangers in the world," a biblical

image (see the words of Moses in Exodus 2:22), and yet the same chapter ends by exhorting the friars to "show that they are members of the same family."

5. What do you make of that?

Reading 3

Here are examples from the life of Francis in which he is shown to reveal that he broke a fast and did other things that were contrary to his usual life of penance. These anecdotes are not unique but are indicative of many similar experiences that people around Francis had of him during his years of ministry. He was often accusing himself—in public—of insincerity, of missing the mark (sin), and of being "less than" what people might think of him.

The Assisi Compilation

Chapter 80
He Avoids Hypocrisy, Confessing What He Has Eaten During an Illness[6]

One time when he had recovered somewhat from a very serious illness, after some consideration, it seemed to him that he had received some little delicacies during that illness, although he ate only a little, since with his many, diverse, and serious illnesses he was not able to eat.

One day, although still sick from a quartan fever, he had the people of Assisi called to the piazza for a sermon. When he had finished preaching, he requested that no one leave until he returned.

---

6.   *Early Documents: Vol. 2 (The Founder)*, 181-82.

Together with Brother Peter of Catanio, whom he chose as the first general minister, and with a few other brothers, he entered the church of San Rufino, going into the *confessio*. He ordered Brother Peter to obey and not contradict whatever he wanted to say and do to himself. And Brother Peter said to him: "Brother, in what concerns you and me, I cannot, and should not want anything else except what pleases you."

Taking off his tunic, blessed Francis ordered Brother Peter to lead him naked with a rope tied around his neck in front of the people. He ordered another brother to take a bowl full of ashes and, mounting the place from where he had preached, to throw them and sprinkle them on his head. But moved by piety and compassion towards him, the brother did not obey him. Brother Peter got up and, weeping bitterly with the other brothers, led him out as he had been ordered to do.

In this way he came back in front of the people naked, to the place where he had preached, and said: "You believe me to be a holy man, as do others who, following my example, leave the world and enter the religion and life of the brothers. But I confess to God and to you that during my illness I ate meat and broth flavored with meat."

Almost all the people began to weep out of piety and compassion for him, especially since it was wintertime and was very cold and he had not yet recovered from the quartan fever. They struck their breasts, accusing themselves. "This holy man," they said, "whose life we know, accuses himself with such shame over a just and manifest necessity. Yet because of excessive abstinence and the severity with which he treats his body from the moment of his conversion to Christ, we see him living in flesh that is almost dead. What shall we do, wretches that we are, we who all our life have lived, and wish to live, according to the will and desires of the flesh?"

Chapter 81
He Abhors Hypocrisy Both in Eating and in Clothing[7]

Likewise, at another time, he was staying in a hermitage for the Lent of Saint Martin. Because of his illness, the brothers cooked the food they gave him to eat in lard, because oil was very bad for him in his illnesses. When the forty days had ended and he was preaching to a large crowd of people, gathered not far from that hermitage, in the opening words of his sermon he told them: "You came to me with great devotion and believe me to be a holy man. But I confess to God and to you that during this Lent in that hermitage, I have eaten food flavored with lard."

Indeed, if the brothers or the friends of the brothers, with whom he would eat, occasionally prepared a special dish for him because of his illnesses or the obvious need of his body, it frequently happened that he would immediately tell this to the brothers or lay people who did not know about it, whether inside the house or outside, saying publicly: "I ate such and such foods." He did not wish to conceal from people what was known to God.

---

7.   *Early Documents: Vol. 2 (The Founder)*, 182-83.

Moreover, if his soul were ever tempted to vainglory, pride, or any vice, no matter where he was, or in whose presence, whether they be religious or lay, he would immediately and openly confess it to them, without concealing anything. That is why he told his companions one day: "I want to live before God, in hermitages and other places where I stay, just as the people see and know me. If they believe that I am a holy man and I do not lead a life becoming a holy man, I would be a hypocrite."

Thus one time in winter, one of the companions, who was his guardian, acquired a piece of fox fur because of the illness of the spleen and the cold of his stomach. He asked him to permit him to have it sewn under his tunic next to his stomach and spleen, especially because it was then extremely cold. But from the moment he began to serve Christ until the day of his death, in any weather, he did not want to wear or have anything but a single patched tunic.

Blessed Francis answered him: "If you want me to wear that fur under the tunic, allow me to sew a piece of the fur on the outside of my tunic as an indication to people that I have a piece of fur underneath." And this is what he had done; and, although it was a necessity on account of his illnesses, he did not wear it long.

Reflect or Discuss

1. In the first selection, what happens in Francis before he makes his public confession? What is it that stirs in him?

2. Why do you think Francis felt his confession needed to be so public?

3. How is the fasting, and the confessing, all part of a life of penance?

4. Considering both selections, notice how Francis is continually gauging and monitoring his levels of comfort and self-care.

5. Read again the last two paragraphs, regarding Francis's tunic and fur used to make it warmer one winter, and ask yourself: What is the meaning of penance?

Reading 4

This selection from Bonaventure's *Major Legend*, the biography Bonaventure wrote about Francis which was meant to replace all the previous ones, demonstrates how Francis was serious in his attention to penance but how he also insisted on moderating personal severity with personal charity.

We also see Francis teaching the virtue of daily and regular work, and not as penance; this is how some others described work, then and now, as a punishment that originated with the sin of Adam and Eve and being expelled from the Garden of Eden. God says to Adam and Eve: "By the sweat of your face you shall eat bread until you return to the ground, for out of it you were taken; you are dust, and to dust you shall return" (Gen 3:19). But, to Francis, work is good for the soul.

Similarly, he advises silence—not because he wants his friars to be like contemplative monks, shut up in monasteries, but again, to guard the heart, to feed the soul, and to steer away from carelessness. The phrase he uses is "shallow talk."

Call them by other names, if you will, but these are forms of penance, and they are penances that are advised because they are good for you.

The Major Legend of Saint Francis
Bonaventure of Bagnoregio

From *Chapter 5*
*The Austerity of His Life and How Creatures
Provided Him Comfort*[8]

He taught the brothers to flee with all their might from idleness, the cesspool of all evil thoughts; and he demonstrated to them by his own example that they should master their rebellious and lazy flesh by constant discipline and useful work. Therefore he used to call his body Brother Ass, for he felt it should be subjected to heavy labor, beaten frequently with whips, and fed with the poorest food.

If he saw someone idle and vagrant, wanting to eat the labors of others, he thought he should be called "Brother Fly," because he did nothing good himself but poisoned the good done by others and so rendered himself useless and obnoxious to all. On account of this he once said: "I want my brothers to work and be kept busy, lest, given to idleness, they stray into what is forbidden with heart and tongue."

He strongly wanted the brothers to observe the silence recommended by the Gospel, so that they particularly abstain at all times from every idle word, since they would have to render an account on the day of judgment. But if he found a brother accustomed to shallow talk, he would reprimand him bitterly, affirming that a modest silence was the guardian of a pure heart and no small virtue itself, in view of the fact that death and life

8.   *Early Documents: Vol. 2 (The Founder)*, 564-65.(corrected)

are said to be in the hands of the tongue, not so much by reason of taste as by reason of speech.

Although he energetically urged the brothers to lead an austere life, he was not pleased by an intransigent severity that did not put on a heart of piety and was not seasoned with the salt of discernment. One night, when one of the brothers was tormented with hunger because of his excessive fasting, he was unable to get any rest. The pious shepherd understood the danger threatening his sheep, called the brother, put some bread before him, and, to take away his embarrassment, he started eating first and gently invited him to eat. The brother put aside his embarrassment, took the food, overjoyed that, through the discerning condescension of his shepherd, he had both avoided harm to his body, and received an edifying example of no small proportion.

When morning came, after the man of God had called the brothers together and recounted what had happened during the night, he added this reminder: "Brothers, in this incident let charity, not food, be an example for you." He taught them, moreover, to follow discernment as the charioteer of the virtues, not that which the flesh recommends, but that taught by Christ, whose most sacred life expressed for us the exemplar of perfection.

Reflect or Discuss

1. What do you think of physical work and voluntary silence as forms of penance?

2. Notice what Francis advises regarding silence, in the life of a Franciscan. Can we do penance both through talking and, sometimes, not talking?

3. Notice how Francis contrasts "intransigent severity" with "a heart of piety." How would you describe these alternative ways of being Christian?

4. How does *carefulness* describe a Lenten approach to life?

5. How does *charity* describe a Lenten approach to life?

Reading 5

To read the full life of Francis is to discover that Francis made mistakes, and not only honorable ones. An honorable mistake might be when a job interviewer asks, "What would you say are your faults?" and you respond, "I'm impatient sometimes. I want to get everything done as quickly as possible." In other words, the mention of the fault is really a way of communicating a strength. In the lives of saints, an honorable fault might be to be so focused on spiritual matters that one forgets to eat, or drink, or sleep.

Francis was at fault in how he treated his body—something he admitted toward the end of his life. He wasn't simply so earnest, so spiritual, that he forgot to eat and drink and care for himself; he sometimes didn't care for himself in ways that were contrary to the teachings of scripture—and he realized it—apparently only after the stigmata experience, when he experienced pain that he clearly felt was divinely sent. This realization of being at fault in the area of penance puts into fuller picture how Lent is a way of life for Christians.

What follows are three selections from two different sources.

A Mirror of the Perfection

Chapter 37[9]

9.   *Early Documents: Vol. 3 (The Prophet)*, 245.

When blessed Francis sent brothers through the regions to preach penance, he said to them: "Go, in the name of the Lord, two by two along the way, decently, in the greatest silence from dawn until after terce, praying to the Lord in your hearts. And let no idle or useless words be mentioned among you. Although you are traveling, nevertheless, let your behavior be as decent as if you were staying in a hermitage or a cell because wherever we are or wherever we travel, we have a cell with us. Brother Body is our cell, and the soul is the hermit who remains inside the cell to pray to God and meditate. So if the soul does not remain in quiet and solitude in its cell, a cell made by hands does little good to a religious."

Chapter 97[10]

The most holy father, realizing and understanding that the body was created for the soul and that bodily needs are to be fulfilled because of spiritual ones, used to say: "In eating, sleeping, and fulfilling other bodily needs, a servant of God must satisfy his body with discernment. In this way Brother Body cannot grumble, saying: 'Because you do not satisfy my needs, I cannot stand up straight and persevere in prayer, or rejoice in tribulations, or do other good works.'

"On the other hand, if a servant of God, with discernment, has satisfied his body well enough, but Brother Body wants to be lazy, negligent, and sleepy in prayer, vigils and other good works, then he should pun-

---

10.   *Early Documents: Vol. 3 (The Prophet),* 344.

ish it like any wicked and lazy beast of burden, because it wants to eat but refuses to work and carry its weight.

"If, however, because of want or poverty, Brother Body, whether healthy or sick, cannot have its needs fulfilled, after he has requested them decently and humbly for the love of God from his brother or his prelate and they are not given to him, then let him patiently bear this for the love of God Who also suffered want and found not one to comfort him. If he bears this need with patience, the Lord will credit it to him as martyrdom. And because he did what is his to do, making his needs known humbly, he would be excused from sin, even if the body on this account became more gravely ill."

The Legend of Three Companions

Chapter 5
How the Crucifix Spoke to Him for the First Time and How He Henceforth Carried the Passion of Christ in His Heart Until Death[11]

[W]hile he was walking by the church of San Damiano, he was told in the Spirit to go inside for a prayer. Once he entered, he began to pray intensely before an image of the Crucified, which spoke to him in a tender and kind voice: "Francis, don't you see that my house is being destroyed? Go, then, and rebuild it for me." Stunned and trembling, he said: "I will do so gladly, Lord." For he understood that it was speaking about that

---

11.   *Early Documents: Vol. 2 (The Founder)*, 76.

church, which was near collapse because of its age. He was filled with such joy and became so radiant with light over that message, that he knew in his soul that it was truly Christ crucified who spoke to him.

Upon leaving the church, he found a priest sitting nearby and, putting his hands into the pouch, he offered him a handful of coins. "My Lord," he said, "I beg you, buy some oil and keep the light before the Crucified burning continually. When this money runs out, I will again give you as much as you need."

From that hour, therefore, his heart was wounded and it melted when remembering the Lord's passion. While he lived, he always carried the wounds of the Lord Jesus in his heart. This was brilliantly shown afterwards in the renewal of those wounds that were miraculously impressed on and most clearly revealed in his body.

From then on, he inflicted his flesh with such fasting that, whether healthy or sick, the excessively austere man hardly ever or never wanted to indulge his body. Because of this he confessed on his death bed that he had greatly sinned against "Brother Body."

Reflect or Discuss

1. How did Francis measure the proper amount of penance as relating to the needs of his body?

2. What did Francis do that might be considered wrong?

3. Consider the teaching of another reformer from the century before Francis: St. Bernard of Clairvaux. Bernard said: "I do not want to say that you should hate your own flesh [see Eph 5:29]. Love it as something given you as a helper and a partner prepared to share in eternal happiness. . . . The soul should love the flesh, but should even more tend her own animate life. Let Adam love his Eve, but he must not love her so much that he obeys her voice rather than God's." (*Sermons on Conversion*, trans. Marie-Bernard Said, OSB; Kalamazoo, MI: Cistercian Publications, 1981; 195.)

4. In what ways do you think St. Francis would agree with St. Bernard?

5. What do you think of referring to your body as "Brother Ass," in other words, as that which carries you from here to there in this life, and as that which often requires being hit with a stick to get moving or doing what it ought to do?

Reading 6

Essential to the Franciscan path is the role of other people in our Christian formation. We don't "go it alone," and we don't relate solely to God in Christ. We need the Church and the sacraments. And we need each other. We rely on each other.

We make promises (and vows—if we're vowed Franciscans) not only to God, and to the Church, but to each other.

This final reading of Week One is advice that Francis gave to his brothers who wanted to live for a time in hermitages, apart from larger friaries of brothers. His advice to them is personal, intimate, detailed, and spiritually and psychologically astute.

A Rule for Hermitages

Francis of Assisi[12]

Let those who wish to stay in hermitages in a religious way be three brothers or, at the most, four; let two of these be "the mother" and have two "sons" or at least one. Let the two who are "mothers" keep the life of Martha and the two "sons" the life of Mary and let one have one enclosure in which each one may have his cell in which he may pray and sleep.

---

12.   *Early Documents: Vol. 1 (The Saint)*, 61-62.

And let them always recite Compline of the day immediately after sunset and strive to maintain silence, recite their Hours, rise for Matins, and seek first the kingdom of God and His justice. And let them recite Prime at the proper hour and, after Terce, they may end their silence, speak with and go to their mothers. And when it pleases them, they can beg alms from them as poor little ones out of love of the Lord God. And afterwards let them recite Sext, None and, at the proper hour, Vespers.

And they may not permit anyone to enter or eat in the enclosure where they dwell. Let those brothers who are the "mothers" strive to stay far from everyone and, because of obedience to their minister, protect their "sons" from everyone so that no one can speak with them. And those "sons" may not talk with anyone except with their "mothers" and with the minister and his custodian when it pleases them to visit with the Lord's blessing.

The "sons," however, may periodically assume the role of the "mothers," taking turns for a time as they have mutually decided. Let them strive to observe conscientiously and eagerly everything mentioned above.

Reflect or Discuss

1. What does Francis mean by being a mother to each other?

2. Read the account in the Gospel of Matthew about Mary and Martha. "Now as they went on their way, he entered a certain village, where a woman named

41

Martha welcomed him into her home. She had a sister named Mary, who sat at the Lord's feet and listened to what he was saying. But Martha was distracted by her many tasks; so she came to him and asked, 'Lord, do you not care that my sister has left me to do all the work by myself? Tell her then to help me.' But the Lord answered her, 'Martha, Martha, you are worried and distracted by many things; there is need of only one thing. Mary has chosen the better part, which will not be taken away from her.'" (Luke 10:38-42)

3. How might the friars in hermitages resemble Mary and Martha?

4. Consider this from St. John of the Cross: "It should be known . . . that God nurtures and caresses the soul, after it has been resolutely converted to his service, like a loving mother who warms her child with the heat of her bosom, nurses it with good milk and tender food, and carries and caresses it in her arms. But as the child grows older, the mother withholds her caresses and hides her tender love; she rubs bitter aloes on her sweet breast and sets the child down from her arms, letting it walk on its own feet so that it may put aside the habits of childhood and grow accustomed to greater and more important things. The grace of God acts just as a loving mother by re-engendering in the soul new enthusiasm and fervor in the service of God." (*The Dark Night of the Soul*)

5. How is God like a mother to us?

Week One Prayer of Intention / Spiritual Practice

Take some time now, alone or with others, to consider what it is that you desire to fast from, and where or how in your life you need to feast more easily. Lent is a season for fasting, and when it is over, we have to remember why we also sometimes feast. Fasting and feasting relate to each other.

From what should you fast?

How might feasting renew you, also?

* * *

You may want to pray these words, which can guide you whether you are fasting or feasting:

What you are doing, may you keep on doing and do not stop.
But with swiftness, agility, and unswerving feet,
    may you go forward with joy and security knowing
    that you are on the path of wisdom and happiness.
Believe nothing, and agree with nothing that will turn you
    away from this commitment.
Nothing should be allowed to prevent you from offering
yourself
    to the Most High in the perfection to which
    the Spirit of God has called you. Amen.

-St. Clare of Assisi[13]

---

13.   From *Lord, Make Me an Instrument of Your Peace: The Complete Prayers of St. Francis, St. Clare, with Selections from Brother Juniper, St. Anthony of Padua, and Other Early Franciscans*, ed. Jon M. Sweeney (Brewster, MA: Paraclete Press, 2020), 120.

Week Two

The Lost Art of Compunction

What is compunction? It's not a word that Francis ever used, but that is not surprising, given that he didn't use many theological words ever. Compunction is a word common in ascetical theology. It means to awaken a spirit of, and feelings of, remorse for sin. Those who are jaded to sin or have grown cynical about the impact of sin on their life are especially in need of compunction.

Compunction is a form of penance: practiced self-consciously and deliberately by the faithful throughout the history of the church.

As both a practice and as a word, compunction has always been more common in the Christian East than in the Christian West. One of the classic texts in the East chanted each year during the Lenten fast is known as The Great Canon of St. Andrew of Crete. The Great Canon includes these lines of prayer:

O Lamb of God,
Who take away the sins of all,
Take from me the heavy yoke of sin,
And in Your compassion
Grant me tears of compunction.

One mourns one's sin, which is separation from God, in order that the tears of mourning might help cleanse one's soul of the sin and heal that separation. St. John Climacus, in the early seventh century, said in *The Ladder of Divine Ascent*, "When our soul leaves this world we shall not be blamed for not having worked miracles, or for not having been theologians or contemplatives. But we shall certainly have to give an account to God of why we have not unceasingly mourned."[14]

In the Western monastic tradition, similar teachings can be found in St. Benedict and his *Rule*. Most memorably, Benedict advises in the lengthy Prologue of the *Rule* how a monk can "with a little severity" over time "enlarge the heart" with love. The whole passage reads like this:

> But if in some things we proceed with a little severity, sound reason so advising, for the amendment of vices or preserving of charity, do not straightway out of fear of this flee from the way of salvation which is always strait and difficult in the beginning.
>
> But in process of time and growth of faith, when the heart has once been enlarged, the way of God's commandments is run with unspeakable sweetness of love.

---

14. John Climacus, *The Ladder of Divine Ascent*, step 7 "on mourning which causes joy," 1, 4, 24-26, 70, translated by Archimandrite Lazarus Moore (New York: Harper & Brothers, 1959).

So that, never departing from His teaching, but persevering in the monastery in His doctrine until death, we share now by patience in the sufferings of Christ, that we may deserve afterwards to be partakers of His kingdom.

One of the most common compunction practices in everyday use by ordinary Christians is the Ignatian practice of a daily Examen. This has become increasingly popular in recent years, but goes back to St. Ignatius himself: a brief reflection on the events of the day in order to realize God's presence in our lives and discern God's direction for tomorrow.

Through practices such as the Examen, we are able, again and again, to return our attention to God. The Catechism of the Catholic Church says: "Conversion is first of all a work of the grace of God who makes our hearts return to him: 'Restore us to thyself, O LORD, that we may be restored!'" (#1432). The scripture there is from Lamentations 5:21.

The word compunction first appears in the Franciscan textual tradition in *The Versified Life of Saint Francis* by Henri d'Avranches, written approximately twenty years after Francis's death:[15]

Rinsing dew the Holy Spirit moistens his [Francis's] faithful heart with;

---

15.   *Francis of Assisi: Early Documents (The Saint)*, 437. There are several scenes like this in the life of Francis.

Compunction, like a broom, sweeping the house
makes it fit

For that Guest.

That's a beautiful image—of the Spirit working in
one's heart like a broom, to make the house fitter for
that same Spirit/God. Still, Francis's own compunction
practices could at times be difficult to emulate, as we will
see. Even Bonaventure said so, in his *Major Legend* of
the saint.

Reading 1

These first two selections around our theme for Week Two reveal Francis's attitude toward the human body in general, and his own body, a topic that is relevant for anyone considering the penance of compunction.

Francis surely never studied the ancient Greek philosophers, but he inherited the understanding in the West since Plato that the passions of the body may have a powerful influence, often detrimental, on the human spirit or soul.

The Major Legend of Saint Francis
Bonaventure of Bagnoregio

From *Chapter Six*
His Humility and Obedience and the Divine Condescensions
Made to Him at His Nod[16]

Once it happened, because he was ill, he somewhat relaxed the rigor of his abstinence in order to recover his health. When his physical strength returned, the authentic scorner of himself was inspired to insult his own flesh. "It is not right," he said, "that people should believe I am abstaining while, in fact, I eat meat secretly." He got up, inflamed with the spirit of true humility, and after he had called the people together in the piazza of the city

---

16.   *Early Documents, Vol. 2 (The Founder)*, 570.

of Assisi, he solemnly entered the principal church with many of the brothers whom he had brought with him. He commanded that he be dragged before the eyes of all, with a cord tied around his neck and stripped to only his underwear, to the stone where criminals received their punishment. Climbing upon the stone, although he had a fever and was weak and the weather was bitter cold, he preached with much vigor and spirit. He asserted to all his hearers that he should not be honored as a spiritual man but rather he should be despised by all as a carnal man and a glutton. Therefore those who had gathered there were amazed at so great a spectacle. They were well aware of his austerity, and so their hearts were struck with compunction; but they professed that his humility was easier to admire than to imitate.

The Remembrance of the Desire of a Soul
Thomas of Celano

The Second Book

Chapter 97
Further Words Against Those Who Praise Themselves[17]

He would often say to the brothers: "No one should flatter himself with big applause for doing something a sinner can do. A sinner can fast," he said, "he can pray, he can weep, he can mortify his flesh. But this he cannot do: remain faithful to his Lord. So this is the only reason

---

17.   *Early Documents: Vol. 2 (The Founder)*, 334.

for boasting: if we return to God the glory that is his; if we serve him faithfully and credit him for what he has given us.

"A person's worst enemy is the flesh; it does not know how to remember what it should regret and it doesn't know how to foresee what it should fear. All its concern is how to squander the present. What is worse," he said, "it claims for itself and takes credit for what was given not to it, but given to the soul. It grabs the praise for virtues and outsiders' applause for vigils and prayers. It leaves nothing for the soul, and even expects to be paid for its tears."

Reflect or Discuss

1. What do you think of what Francis did, in the first scene?

2. How is the spirit of compunction demonstrated in him?

3. What else do you see in him, in that first selection?

4. In the second selection, what does Francis teach about the human body?

5. Do you think he was right in what he said? Why or why not?

Reading 2

Compunction is uncommon today because we are uncomfortable with the idea of berating ourselves. This is understandable; there has been so much self-abuse, and we've heard and read about examples of penance that border on madness. We also have grown increasingly uncomfortable with metaphors for God that center on God's sovereignty and royalty—metaphors that seem to demand acts of lowliness and servitude on our part. These metaphors have been common in our liturgies and prayers for two thousand years; only quite recently have we begun to remove, replace, or modify them.

Nevertheless, compunction has its place in a Lenten life. Francis believed in this wholeheartedly. There are compunction practices that are safe, healthy, and essential for a Christian. That said, Francis didn't always practice his own compunction in these healthy and whole ways. He went overboard, at times, physically and spiritually.

Consider this portion from the first *Life of Saint Francis* written by Thomas of Celano:

Chapter 19
His Watchfulness Over the Brothers, Scorn for Himself, and
True Humility[18]

---

18.   *Early Documents, Vol. 1 (The Saint)*, 227-29.

Blessed Francis returned in body to his brothers, whom, as was said above, he never left in spirit. Asking carefully and in detail about all their doings, he was always moved by a wholesome curiosity about those in his charge. If he found something inappropriate was done, he did not leave it unpunished. He first discerned any spiritual vices. Then he judged those of the body, and finally uprooted any occasions that might open the way to sin.

He zealously and carefully safeguarded Lady Holy Poverty. In order to avoid the superfluous, he would not even permit a small plate to remain in the house if, without it, he could avoid dire need. He said it was impossible to satisfy necessity without bowing to pleasure. He rarely or hardly ever ate cooked foods, but if he did, he would sprinkle them with ashes or dampen the flavor of spices with cold water. Often, when he was wandering through the world to preach the gospel of God, he was called to a dinner given by great princes who venerated him with much fondness. He would taste some meat in order to observe the holy gospel. The rest, which he appeared to eat, he put in his lap, raising his hand to his mouth so that no one could know what he was doing. What shall I say about drinking wine, when he would not allow himself to drink even enough water when he was burning with thirst?

Now as to his bed: wherever he received hospitality, he refused to use a straw mattress or blankets. The naked ground received his naked body, with only a thin tunic between them. Sometimes when he would refresh his small body with sleep, he would often sleep sitting up, not lying down, using a stone or a piece of wood as a pillow.

As normally happens, sometimes the craving to eat something came upon him, but afterwards he would barely allow himself to eat it. Once, because he was ill, he ate a little bit of chicken. When his physical strength returned, he entered the city of Assisi. When he reached the city gate, he commanded the brother who was with him to tie a cord around his neck and drag him through the whole city as if he were a thief, loudly crying out: "Look! See this glutton who grew fat on the flesh of chickens that he ate without your knowledge." Many people ran to see this grand spectacle and, groaning and weeping, they said: "Woe to us! We are wretches and our whole life is steeped in blood! With excess and drunkenness we feed our hearts and bodies to over-flowing!" They were touched in their hearts and were moved to a better way of life by such an example.

He often did things in this way both to despise himself fully and to invite others to everlasting honors. Toward himself he had become like a broken vessel, burdened by no fear or concern for his body. He would zealously expose himself to insults so that he would not be forced by self-love to lust for anything temporal. A true scorner of himself, he taught others to despise themselves by word and example. To what end? He was honored by all and merited high marks from everyone. He alone considered himself vile and was the only one to despise himself fervently. Often honored by others, he suffered great sorrow. Shunning human praise, he had someone, as an antidote, revile him. He would call one of the brothers to him, saying, "I command you under obedience to insult me harshly and speak the truth against their lies." When the brother, though unwilling, called him a boor and a useless hired-hand, he would smile and clap loudly, saying: "May the Lord bless you, for you are really telling the truth; that is what the son of Pietro Bernardone needs to hear." Speaking in this fashion, he called to mind the humble origins of his birth.

In order to show himself contemptible and to give others an example of true confession, when he did something wrong he was not ashamed to confess it in his preaching before all the people. In fact, if he had perhaps thought ill of someone or for some reason let slip a harsh word, he would go with all humility to the person of whom he had said or thought something wrong and, confessing his sin, would ask forgiveness. His conscience, a witness of total innocence, guarding itself with all care, would not let him rest until it gently healed the wound of his heart. In every type of praiseworthy deed he wished to be outstanding, but to go unnoticed. In every way he fled praise to avoid all vanity.

> Woe to us who have now lost you,
> O worthy father,
> model of all kindness and humility!
> Since we did not strive to know you when we had you,
> we have lost you by a just judgment!

* * *

It is probably safe to say that his personal severity would make most people uncomfortable today. Consider this portion from St. Bonaventure:

The Major Legend of Saint Francis

From *Chapter 6*
His Humility and Obedience and the Divine Condescen-
sions Made to Him at His Nod[19]

Humility,
the guardian and embellishment of all the virtues,
had filled the man of God with abundance.
In his own opinion
he was nothing but a sinner,
though in truth he was a mirror
and the splendor of every kind of holiness.
As he had learned from Christ,
he strove to build himself upon this
like a wise architect laying a foundation.
He used to say that it was for this reason
that the Son of God came down
from the height of his Father's bosom
to our lowly estate
so that our Lord and Teacher might teach humility
in both example and word.

Therefore as Christ's disciple, he strove to regard
himself as worthless in his own eyes and those of others,
recalling what had been said by his supreme Teacher:
What is highly esteemed among mortals is an abomina-
tion before God. He used to make this statement frequently: "What a person is before God, that he is and no

---

19.   *Early Documents, Vol. 2 (The Founder)*, 569-71.

more." Therefore, judging that it was foolish to be elated by worldly favors, he rejoiced in insults and was saddened by praise. If nothing else, he would rather hear himself blamed than praised, knowing that the former would lead him to change his life, while the latter would push him to a fall. And so frequently when people extolled the merits of his holiness, he commanded one of the brothers to impress upon his ears words that were, on the contrary, insulting. When the brother, though unwilling, called him a boor and a mercenary, unskilled and useless, he would reply, exhilarated in mind and face: "May the Lord bless you, my beloved son, for it is you who are really telling the very truth and what the son of Peter Bernardone needs to hear."

In order to make himself looked down upon by others,
he did not spare himself the shame of bringing up his
own faults
in his preaching before all the people.

Once it happened, because he was ill, he somewhat relaxed the rigor of his abstinence in order to recover his health. When his physical strength returned, the authentic scorner of himself was inspired to insult his own flesh. "It is not right," he said, "that people should believe I am abstaining while, in fact, I eat meat secretly." He got up, inflamed with the spirit of true humility, and after he had called the people together in the piazza of the city of Assisi, he solemnly entered the principal church with many of the brothers whom he had brought with him. He commanded that he be dragged before the eyes of all, with a cord tied around his neck and stripped to only his underwear, to the stone where criminals received their punishment. Climbing upon the stone, although he had a fever and was weak and the weather was bitter cold, he preached with much vigor and spirit. He asserted to all his hearers that he should not be honored as a spiritual man but rather he should be despised by all as a carnal man and a glutton. Therefore those who had gathered there were amazed at so great a spectacle. They were well aware of his austerity, and so their hearts were struck with compunction; but they professed that his humility was easier to admire than to imitate. Although this incident seemed to be more a portent like that of a prophetic utterance than an example, nevertheless it was a lesson in true humility instructing the follower of Christ that he must condemn the fame of transitory praise, suppress the arrogance of bloated bragging, and reject the lies of deceptive pretense.

He more often did many things in this way,
that outwardly he would become like a discarded utensil
while inwardly he would possess the spirit of holiness.

He strove to hide the good things of his Lord in the secrecy of his heart, not wanting to display for his own glory what could be the cause of ruin. For often, when many were calling him blessed, he would utter words of this sort: "Don't praise me as if I were safe! I can still have sons and daughters. No one should be praised as long as his end is uncertain." This he would say to those who praised him; but to himself: "Francis, if the Most

High had given so much to a thief, he would be more grateful than you!"

He would often say to the brothers: "No one should flatter himself for big applause for doing anything a sinner can do. A sinner," he said, "can fast, pray, weep, and mortify his flesh. This one thing he cannot do: be faithful to his Lord. So this is the only reason for boasting: if we return to the Lord the glory that is his, if we serve him faithfully, and credit Him for what he has given us."

Reflect or Discuss

1. Does all of this penitent behavior make you uncomfortable? Why or why not?

2. Would you do similar sorts of things, as part of your faith? Why or why not?

3. What does it mean to be praised? To be flattered?

4. What does it mean to praise or flatter oneself? Is this ever good?

5. How else can the need for praise be satisfied?

Reading 3

In his compunction, and about his compunction, Francis remained mostly silent. One doesn't usually talk about gifts of things like tears, and perhaps tears are given by God precisely to those who sorrow for their sins humbly and privately. It is also perhaps indiscreet to talk much about contemplating one's death; it isn't something to chat about.

We began to see this at the tail-end of the second portion of Reading 2: Francis didn't seek to share with his friends what he was hearing from God, or what he was expunging from his soul, even though he urged those who were trying to follow his way of life to be likewise vigilant. He wanted to keep these things secret.

Witness, now, this representative passage from Thomas of Celano's *Life of Saint Francis*:

Chapter 3
How, Changed in Mind but Not in Body,
Francis Talked Allegorically About the Treasure He Had
Found
And About His Bride[20]

Changed in mind but not in body, he now refused to go to Apulia and was anxious to direct his will to God's. Thus he retired for a short time from the tumult

---

20. *Early Documents, Vol. 1 (The Saint)*, 187-88.

and business of the world and was anxious to keep Jesus Christ in his inmost self. Like an experienced merchant, he concealed the pearl he had found from the eyes of mockers and selling all he had, he tried to buy it secretly.

Now there was in the city of Assisi a man he loved more than all the rest. They were of the same age and the constant intimacy of their mutual love made him bold to share his secrets with him. He often brought him to remote places suitable for talking, asserting that he had found a great and valuable treasure. This man was overjoyed, and since he was so excited about what he heard, he gladly went with him whenever he was summoned. There was a cave near the city where they often went and talked together about the treasure. The man of God, who was already holy because of his holy intention, was accustomed to enter the cave, while his companion waited outside, and inspired by a new and extraordinary spirit he would pray to his Father in secret. He acted in such a way that no one would know what was happening within. Wisely taking the occasion of the good to conceal the better, he consulted God alone about his holy purpose. He prayed with all his heart that the eternal and true God guide his way and teach him to do His will. He endured great suffering in his soul, and he was not able to rest until he accomplished in action what he had conceived in his heart. Different thoughts followed one after another, and their relentlessness severely disturbed him. He was burning inwardly with a divine fire, and he was unable to conceal outwardly the flame kindled in his soul. He repented that he had sinned so grievously and that he had offended the eyes of majesty. While his past and present transgressions no longer delighted him, he was not yet fully confident of refraining from future ones. Therefore, when he came back out to his companion, he was so exhausted from his struggle that one person seemed to have entered, and another to have come out.

One day, when he had invoked the Lord's mercy with his whole heart, the Lord showed him what he must do. He was filled with such great joy that, failing to restrain himself in the face of his happiness, he carelessly mentioned something to others. Even though he could not remain silent because of the greatness of the love inspired in him, he nevertheless spoke cautiously and in riddles. Just as he spoke to his special friend about a hidden treasure, so he endeavored to talk to others in figures of speech. He said that he did not want to go to Apulia, but promised to do great and noble deeds at home. People thought he wanted to get married, and they would ask him: "Do you want to get married, Francis?" He replied: "I will take a bride more noble and more beautiful than you have ever seen, and she will surpass the rest in beauty and excel all others in wisdom."

Reflect or Discuss

1. This was early in Francis's conversion, before he gave away everything he had in the world. It says, he "was anxious to keep Jesus Christ in his inmost self." Why would that be?

2. Read Matthew, chapter 13. Jesus says: "The kingdom of heaven is like treasure hidden in a field,

which someone found and hid; then in his joy he goes and sells all that he has and buys that field." (Mt 13:44)

3. Why find the treasure and then hide it?

4. Can you think of other passages from scripture that relate to quietness or secrecy as part of the spiritual life?

5. Why would Jesus speak in parables? Why would Francis, as in this passage, speak in riddles?

Reading 4

Again, we look to a portion from Thomas of Celano's *Life of Saint Francis*, and this time we have a closer glimpse of Francis's prayer practice in secret.

He seems to practice what we've come to know as the Jesus Prayer—more common today in Eastern Christianity than in Western Christianity. It traditionally goes, "Lord Jesus Christ, Son of God, have mercy on me, a sinner." This simple prayer—which is sometimes even shortened further—is repeated over and over until, hopefully, it might begin to reverberate in the heart of the person praying, like a heartbeat, the pray-er no longer even needing to vocalize it or think its words.

The Life of Saint Francis
Thomas of Celano

Chapter 11
The Spirit of Prophecy and the
Admonitions of Saint Francis[21]

Day by day the blessed father Francis was being filled with the consolation and the grace of the Holy Spirit, and, with all vigilance and concern, he was forming his new sons with new instruction, teaching them

---

21.   *Early Documents, Vol. 1 (The Saint)*, 205-06.

to walk with steady steps the way of holy poverty and blessed simplicity.

One day he was marveling at the Lord's mercy in the kindness shown to him. He wished that the Lord would show him the course of life for him and his brothers, and he went to a place of prayer, as he so often did. He remained there a long time with fear and trembling before the Ruler of the whole earth. He recalled in the bitterness of his soul the years he spent badly, frequently repeating this phrase: "Lord, be merciful to me, a sinner." Gradually, an indescribable joy and tremendous sweetness began to well up deep in his heart.

He began to lose himself;
his feelings were pressed together; and that darkness
disappeared
which fear of sin had gathered in his heart.
Certainty of the forgiveness of all his sins poured in,
and the assurance of being revived in grace was given to
him.
Then he was caught up above himself and totally
engulfed in light,
and, with his inmost soul opened wide,
he clearly saw the future.
As that sweetness and light withdrew,
renewed in spirit,
he now seemed to be changed into another man.

He returned and said to the brothers with joy: "Be strong, dear brothers, and rejoice in the Lord. Do not be sad, because you seem so few, and do not let my simplicity or yours discourage you. The Lord has shown me that God will make us grow into a great multitude, and will spread us to the ends of the earth. I must also tell you what I saw about your future, though it would please me more to remain silent, if charity did not compel me to tell you. I saw a great multitude of people coming to us, wishing to live with us in the habit of a holy way of life and in the rule of blessed religion. Listen! The sound of them is still in my ears, their coming and going according to the command of holy obedience. I seemed to see highways filled with this multitude gathering in this region from nearly every nation. Frenchmen are coming, Spaniards are hurrying, Germans and Englishmen are running, and a huge crowd speaking other languages is rapidly approaching."

When the brothers heard this, they were filled with wholesome joy, either because of the grace which the Lord God had conferred on His holy one, or because they eagerly thirsted for the profit of their neighbors, whom they wanted to increase in number daily in order to be saved.

And the holy man said to them: "So that we may give thanks faithfully and devotedly to the Lord our God for all His gifts and that you may know how our present and future brothers should live, understand this truth about the course of things to come. In the beginning of our way of life together we will find fruit that is very sweet and pleasant. A little later fruit that is less pleasant and sweet will be offered. Finally, fruit full of bitterness will be served, which we will not be able to eat. Although displaying some outward beauty and fragrance, it will be too sour for anyone to eat. As I told you, the Lord certainly will make us grow into a great nation. But in the end it will turn out as follows: it is like a man who tosses his nets into the sea or a lake and catches a great number of fish. When he has loaded them all into his boat, he is reluctant to carry them all because of their great number. So he would pick out for his baskets the larger ones and those he likes, but the others he would throw out."

Reflect or Discuss

1. Celano says of Francis: "Certainty of the forgiveness of all his sins poured in, and the assurance of being revived in grace was given to him." Reflect on the sequential nature of these lines: what happens first? What happens second?

2. Notice the repetition of the word "day" in these accounts. What does this imply about Francis's spiritual practice?

3. Compare the last paragraph, and the parable Francis tells of the fish and the fisherman, to the teaching of Jesus from Matthew 13:47-48: "[T]he kingdom of heaven is like a net that was thrown into the sea and caught fish of every kind; when it was full, they drew it ashore, sat down, and put the good into baskets but threw out the bad."

4. How does Francis's teaching on penance and compunction fit with his teachings, or Jesus's teachings, on grace and forgiveness?

5. How do these teachings fit together in a Christian life? A Lenten life?

Reading 5

Avoiding *acedia* was of utmost concern to Francis. He learned this from the great monastic writers of the ancient period and the Middle Ages who warned anyone in religious life against the indifference and laziness, boredom and torpor—that is, *acedia*. The word itself, which has Greek origins, means literally "not caring." In the early fifth century, the monk-writer John Cassian called it "the noonday demon."

Most writers, including St. Benedict, equated *acedia* with one of the seven deadly sins: sloth. In the early sixth century, Benedict opened chapter forty-eight of his *Rule*, "The Daily Manual Labor," saying: "Idleness [*acedia*] is the enemy of the soul."[22] "Weariness in the face of work," the eighth century monk, John of Damascus called it, and by work he meant the responsibilities of prayer and other regular spiritual practice.

The following three episodes reveal this vividly.[23]

The Remembrance of the Desire of a Soul
Thomas of Celano

The Second Book

Chapter 87
A Brother Freed from Temptation

---

22. *The Rule of Saint Benedict in English*, Fry; 47.
23. *Early Documents, Vol. 2 (The Founder)*, 329-30, 331-32.

A certain brother, a spiritual man, an elder in religion, was afflicted with a great tribulation of the flesh, and seemed to be swallowed into the depth of despair. His sorrow doubled daily, as his conscience, more delicate than discerning, made him go to confession over nothing. Certainly there is no need to confess having a temptation, but only giving in to it, even a little. But he was so shamed that he was afraid to reveal the whole thing, even though it was nothing, to a single priest. Instead, dividing up these thoughts, he confided different pieces to different priests. One day as he was walking with blessed Francis, the saint said to him: "Brother, I tell you that from now on you do not have to confess your tribulation to anyone. Do not be afraid. Whatever happens to you that is not your doing will not be to your blame, but to your credit. Whenever you are troubled, I give you my permission just to say seven Our Fathers." The brother wondered how the saint could have known about this; smiling and over- joyed, he got over the temptation in a short time.

Chapter 88
Spiritual Joy and Its Praise and the Evils of Acedia

This holy man insisted that spiritual joy was an infallible remedy against a thousand snares and tricks of the enemy. He used to say: "The devil is most delighted when he can steal the joy of spirit from a servant of God. He carries dust which he tries to throw into the tiniest openings of the conscience, to dirty a clear mind and a clean life. But if spiritual joy fills the heart, the serpent casts its poison in vain. The devils cannot harm a servant of Christ when they see him filled with holy cheerfulness. But when the spirit is teary-eyed, feeling abandoned and sad, it will easily be swallowed up in sorrow, or else be carried away toward empty enjoyment." The saint therefore always strove to keep a joyful heart, to preserve the anointing of the spirit and the oil of gladness.

He avoided very carefully the dangerous disease of *acedia*, so that when he felt even a little of it slipping into his heart, he quickly rushed to prayer. For he used to say: "When a servant of God gets disturbed about something, as often happens, he must get up at once to pray and remain before the most High Father until he gives back to him the joy of his salvation. But if he delays, staying in sadness, that Babylonian sickness will grow and, unless scrubbed with tears, it will produce in the heart permanent rust."

Chapter 92
How the Body Should Be Treated
That It Will Not Complain

The saint also said on one occasion: "Brother Body should be cared for with discernment, so that it won't raise the storm of *acedia*. We must take away from it the occasions for complaining, so it won't get weary keeping vigil and staying reverently at prayer. Otherwise it will say: 'I'm dying of hunger. I can't hold up the load of your exercises.' Now, if it grumbles that way after it has gobbled down a sufficient ration, then you will know that lazy ass needs a good kick, and the reluctant donkey is waiting for the stick."

This was the only teaching in which the most holy father's actions were not in harmony with his words. For he tamed his innocent body with flogging and privation, covering it with wounds for no reason. For the burning of his spirit had already refined his body so much that his most holy flesh thirsted for God in many ways, just as did his soul.

Reflect or Discuss

1. What does Francis prescribe for the man, the "elder in religion," to do to combat his recurring experiences of despair?

2. In the second of the three selections, we have another instance of tears. The subject seems complicated: Look to the first paragraph and the mention of the spirit becoming "teary-eyed" and compare that to the mention in the paragraph that follows, when tears are said to "scrub" sadness.

3. So, are there good and bad tears? How would you describe the difference between the two?

4. How does Francis speak of considering the body when it comes to prayer and spiritual practice?

5. Do you think it's appropriate to give one's "lazy ass" body "a good kick" on occasion? Or is this a teaching to be discontinued?

Reading 6

Ultimately, a Christian undergoes the discipline of compunction as if standing before the Lord Christ himself. This is the essence of what can only be described as the pleading that Francis does with his fellow friars in this address written after he'd stepped down from leadership, and in the year before his death.

Notice the attention to speaking the very name of Christ, and what Francis asks of the friar's body.

Notice the connection he draws between hearing with one's ears and schooling one's heart: the essence of compunction.

Notice how he pleads with the friars who are priests—Francis was not a priest—to reverence the Holy Eucharist.

From *A Letter to the Entire Order*

Francis of Assisi[24]

In the name of the most high Trinity and holy Unity: the Father and the Son and the Holy Spirit.

To all my reverend and dearly beloved brothers: to Brother A., the General Minister of the Order of Friars Minor, its lord, and the other general ministers who

---

24.   *Early Documents: Vol. 1 (The Saint)*, 116-17.

will come after him, and to the ministers, custodians, humble priests of this same brotherhood in Christ, and to all simple and obedient brothers, from the first to the last: Brother Francis, a worthless and weak man, your very little servant sends his greetings in Him Who has redeemed and washed us in His most precious blood. When you hear His name, the name of that Son of the Most High, our Lord Jesus Christ, Who is blessed forever, adore His name with fear and reverence, prostrate on the ground!

Listen, sons of the Lord and my brothers, pay attention to my words. Incline the ear of your heart and obey the voice of the Son of God. Observe His commands with your whole heart and fulfill His counsels with a perfect mind. Give praise to Him because He is good; exalt Him by your deeds; for this reason He has sent you into the whole world: that you may bear witness to His voice in word and deed and bring everyone to know that there is no one who is all-powerful except Him. Persevere in discipline and holy obedience and, with a good and firm purpose, fulfill what you have promised Him. The Lord God offers Himself to us as to His children.

Kissing your feet, therefore, and with all that love of which I am capable, I implore all of you brothers to show all possible reverence and honor to the most holy Body and Blood of our Lord Jesus Christ in Whom that which is in heaven and on earth has been brought to peace and reconciled to almighty God.

I also beg in the Lord all my brothers who are priests, or who will be, or who wish to be priests of the Most High that whenever they wish to celebrate Mass, being pure, they offer the true Sacrifice of the most holy Body and Blood of our Lord Jesus Christ with purity and reverence, with a holy and unblemished intention, not for any worldly reason or out of fear or love of anyone, as if they were pleasing people. But let all their will, as much as grace helps, be directed to God, desiring, thereby, to please only the Most High Lord Himself because He alone acts there as He pleases, for He Himself says: Do this in memory of me. If anyone acts differently, he becomes Judas the traitor and guilty of the Body and Blood of the Lord.

My priest brothers, remember what is written in the law of Moses: whoever committed a transgression against even externals died without mercy by a decree of the Lord. How much greater and more severe will the punishment be of the one who tramples on the Son of God, and who treats the Blood of the Covenant in which he was sanctified as unclean and who insults the Spirit of grace? For a person looks down upon, defiles and tramples upon the Lamb of God when, as the Apostle says, not distinguishing and discerning the holy bread of Christ from other foods or actions, he either unworthily or, even if he is worthy, eats It in vain and unworthily since the Lord says through the prophet: The person is cursed who does the work of the Lord deceitfully. He will, in truth, condemn priests who do not wish to take this to heart, saying: I will curse your blessings.

At the end of this document (the reading above is a portion of the whole), comes perhaps the most beautiful prayer that Francis wrote. It is a summary of praise to be said by the repentant heart:[25]

Almighty, eternal, just and merciful God, give us
miserable ones
the grace to do for You alone what we know you want
us to do
and always to desire what pleases You.
Inwardly cleansed, interiorly enlightened
and inflamed by the fire of the Holy Spirit,
may we be able to follow
in the footprints of Your beloved Son, our Lord Jesus
Christ,
and, by Your grace alone,
may we make our way to You, Most High,
Who live and rule
in perfect Trinity and simple Unity, and are glorified
God almighty, forever and ever.
Amen.

Reflect or Discuss

1. How does this passage from Francis highlight the importance of compunction? How does it demonstrate compunction's urgency for a Christian life?

---

25. *Early Documents: Vol. 1 (The Saint)*, 120-21.

2. In the closing prayer, look again at the words "cleansed," "enlightened," and "inflamed." How do these words relate to what compunction does?

3. What other words might describe the lost art of compunction?

4. Does the broader spiritual term of "mindfulness," common in Buddhism, capture some of what compunction demands?

5. In what ways is "mindfulness" not a complete description of what compunction is about?

Week Two Prayer of Intention / Spiritual Practice

Practice praying now with a spirit of compunction. This may be new to you. It is okay if you feel uncertain how to begin, and if you don't know what to say. Who knows exactly what to say before God? None of us.

Nevertheless, here is a lengthy, substantive prayer, written by a Capuchin Franciscan in 2012, that may give you the words you need:

Prayer of Compunction and Adoration

> Most High, good and loving God, there are so many things for which I used to pray. But now I just don't anymore.

> I used to pray for forgiveness of my sins. But now I don't, because I know that you are the merciful and forgiving God, and if I don't feel forgiven it's because, in my hardness of heart, I have not accepted the vulnerability and humility of receiving your mercy. Or perhaps I have not forgiven from my heart my brother who has sinned against me.

> I used to pray for the graces to overcome the sins that weaken my life with you and hurt my soul. But now I don't, because so many times I have thus prayed in vain, asking wrongly, to

spend it on the passions (James 4:3). For I
didn't want to overcome sin in order to give you
glory, but for the vainglory of thinking myself
devout and holy.

I used to pray to know the next steps in the
journey, both in exterior life and in the interior
journey of prayer. But now I don't. Since I have
not yet fulfilled what you command publicly
and plainly in your Scriptures, loving you with
all my heart and caring for your poor, what
business do I have asking for further, personal
instructions?

So many times I have constructed clever personal tales that recount the work of your grace
over my life, emphasizing unimportant details
that appealed to my vanity and paying no mind
to what you were really doing. Since I have
been unable to interpret clearly the work of
your grace in the past, what makes me think
I understand it well enough in the present to
presume to direct it? Most of the time I have
been for you like an anesthetized patient,
dreaming pious theater while you were at work
on my soul in some way from which I was more
or less distracted.

So I just pray that you keep at it.

I pray also for conversion, for I know it is your
will that I be converted. I pray that my heart and

mind be converted to you, that my thoughts and hands be converted to the salvation you give to my brothers and sisters, especially your poor.

But most of all I pray in thanksgiving. For I know that the whole mess of my being, the meager bits of good that I have let you accomplish in me together with all the misery I insist upon for myself—and my neighbor—with my sins, you take to yourself in the broken Body of Christ crucified. And I know that, on all the altars in all your churches throughout the world—with a humility so deep that it shrouds how it works from our proud minds—you make that broken Body nourishment and salvation for me and for the world.

And for that I adore you.

-Fr. Charles, OFM, Cap[26]

---

26. See https://friarminor.blogspot.com/2012/12/prayer-of-compunc-tion-and-adoration.html. Used by permission of the author.

Week Three

Spending Time Alone

Solitude tends to come when we don't want it, and then to be elusive when we need it most. Prisoners often have solitude in spades and would rather not. Parents with young children end up craving it.

Catholicism has always valued solitude, and some our monastic traditions began with devotion to lives of solitude and prayer. Both Protestantism and the Enlightenment challenged these practices. First, the Protestant reformers (e.g., Martin Luther), and then Enlightenment philosophers (e.g., Denis Diderot), pointed to monks in monasteries, nuns in convents, and even the vow of celibacy itself, denouncing all, suggesting that they are anti-social, dangerous behaviors. Diderot said in 1765: "A solitary is, in regard to the rest of mankind, like an inanimate being; his prayers and his contemplative life, which no one sees, have no influence on society which has more need of examples of virtue before its eyes than in the forests." That stigma remained in Western culture until quite recently.[27]

---

27. Diderot in *A History of Solitude*, by David Vincent (Medford, MA: Polity Press, 2020), 4. With Anthony Storr's *Solitude: A Return to the Self* (New York: Ballantine Books, 1989), views of solitaries and solitude began to change in American culture.

The last three-plus decades have seen a rediscovery of what for many centuries Catholic religious already knew: to spend time alone does not equal being lonely; solitude is an opportunity to quiet one's inner turmoil and noise in order to listen for the presence of God. By doing that, a person learns in and from solitude how to be present for the lives, and in the lives, of others. This is a valuable lesson to learn during Lent, and in order to make our lives more generally Lenten.

However, spending time alone is a form of penance—perhaps, increasingly so in our lives. Most of us can plot ourselves as introverts or extroverts in our Enneagram types or on the Myers-Briggs scale, and this helps us understand how much we do or don't enjoy solitude. But regardless of our personal leanings, even the most ardent introvert tends to spend less and less time in quiet today. We all entertain ourselves so easily, and too frequently, as an escape from stress and responsibilities. We use entertainment—what we used to think of as harmless, simple noise—to divert our attention more than people ever before had been able to do.

If I had to guess based on the evidence we possess, I would say that Francis was somewhere in the middle on the extrovert-introvert spectrum. He loved to be with others, and even to entertain them, singing, dancing, talking, but he also craved time alone. We know, for instance, that early in his conversion he asked two friends, Sylvester and Clare, for advice as to whether his vocation was to be a Christian solitary, devoted to prayer, or what became the Franciscan friar, devoted to accompanying others on the way of conversion. Together, the three of them determined God's will for Francis's life, and the friar was born.

However, Francis purposefully spent time alone again and again, throughout his very active, others-centered life, as a remedy for the noise that can crowd out the presence of God.

Reading 1

Last week we saw how during Francis's conversion he began to spend time alone in a cave with God, and then was hesitant even to tell his best friend what he was experiencing while alone there. It seems that solitude was essential for Francis, given the trajectory of his life up until the time when he began to hear God's voice. He had been busy and gregarious, active and ambitious—all good qualities—but one gets the sense from studying his life that all of this activity and "noise" kept him from discovering who he truly was.

When Francis began to be quiet, as in those times in a cave in solitary prayer, he began to change in many ways. And then, interestingly, Francis remained jealously protective of what he discovered during those quiet times alone with his Lord. He continued to keep what he heard from God, in that quiet, mostly to himself.

The Major Legend of Saint Francis
Bonaventure of Bagnoregio

From *Chapter Six*
His Humility and Obedience and the Divine Condescen-
sions
Made to Him at His Nod[28]

---

28.   *Early Documents, Vol. 2 (The Founder)*, 570-71.

[O]utwardly he [sought to] become like a discarded utensil while inwardly he would possess the spirit of holiness.

He strove to hide the good things of his Lord in the secrecy of his heart, not wanting to display for his own glory what could be the cause of ruin. For often, when many were calling him blessed, he would utter words of this sort: "Don't praise me as if I were safe! I can still have sons and daughters. No one should be praised as long as his end is uncertain." This he would say to those who praised him; but to himself: "Francis, if the Most High had given so much to a thief, he would be more grateful than you!"

He would often say to the brothers: "No one should flatter himself for big applause for doing anything a sinner can do. A sinner," he said, "can fast, pray, weep, and mortify his flesh. This one thing he cannot do: be faithful to his Lord. So this is the only reason for boasting: if we return to the Lord the glory that is his, if we serve him faithfully, and credit Him for what he has given us."

> That this Gospel merchant
> would profit in many ways
> and melt down all the present time into merit,
> he chose not only to be under, rather than above
> but also to obey, rather than command.

Therefore, resigning the office as general, he asked for a guardian whose will he would obey in all things. He maintained that the fruit of holy obedience was so abundant, that, for those who submit their necks to its yoke, no time passes without profit. Therefore he always promised obedience to the brother who customarily was with him when travelling. Once he said to his companions: "Among the many other things that divine piety has bestowed upon me, it has granted me this grace: that I would obey a novice of one hour, if he were given to me as my guardian, as diligently as I would obey the oldest and most discerning brother. A subject," he said, "must not consider in his prelate a human being, but rather Him for love of Whom he is a subject. The more contemptibly he presides, the more pleasing is the humility of the one who obeys."

One time, when they asked him who should be judged truly obedient, he suggested as an example the likeness of a dead body. "Take a lifeless corpse," he said, "and place it wherever you want! You will see that it does not resist being moved, nor complain about location, nor protest if left. Sit it on a throne, and it will look down, not up; dress it in purple, and it looks twice as pale. This," he said, "is someone truly obedient, who doesn't argue about why he's being moved; he doesn't care where he's placed, he doesn't pester you to transfer him. When raised to an office, he keeps his usual humility; the more he's honored, the more he considers himself unworthy."

Reflect or Discuss:

1. What is the connection between humility and secrecy?

2. What is the connection between humility and self-criticism?

3. What is the connection between humility and obedience?

4. How does Francis show his obedience in concrete ways?

5. How does Francis show humility? Can you relate to any of these ways?

Reading 2

Here are two accounts from Francis's life when he sought to spend time alone with God, one from when he was still a young man living in his parents' home and the stirrings of his conversion were beginning to change his behavior. The other is from years later, in his spiritual maturity: the account of a Lenten fast.

The Legend of Three Companions

From *Chapter 3*

How the Lord Visited Francis's Heart for the First Time Filling It with Marvelous Tenderness that Gave Him Strength to Begin to Progress Spiritually in Looking Down on Himself and All Vanities, in Prayer, Almsgiving, and Poverty[29]

[H]e was so accustomed to setting his heart on joining his companions when they called him, and was so captivated by their company, that he would frequently leave the table even if he had eaten only a little. In this way he would upset his parents by his thoughtless flight. Now, however, his whole heart was intent on seeing the poor, listening to them, and giving them alms.

---

29.   *Early Documents: Vol. 2 (The Founder)*, 73-4.

He was so changed by divine grace that, although he was still in secular attire, he yearned to be in another city where, as someone unknown, he would take off his own clothes and, in exchange, put on the rags of a poor man. And he would try begging alms for the love of God.

At this time he happened to go to Rome on pilgrimage. As he was entering the church of Saint Peter, he noticed the meager offerings made by some, and said to himself: "Since the Prince of the Apostles should be greatly honored, why do they make such meager offerings in the church where his body rests?" With great enthusiasm, he took a handful of coins from his money pouch, and threw them through a grating of the altar, making such a loud noise that all the bystanders were astonished at his generosity.

As he was leaving and passed the doors of the church, where there were many poor people begging alms, he secretly exchanged clothes with one of those poor people and put them on. Standing on the steps of the church with the other poor, he begged for alms in French, because he would speak French spontaneously, although he did not do so correctly.

After taking off the beggar's clothes and putting on his own, he returned to Assisi, and began to pray that the Lord would direct his way. He did not share his secret with anyone; nor did he seek counsel from anyone, except from God alone, and, periodically, from the bishop of Assisi. For at that time no one possessed the real poverty that he desired more than anything else in this world, in which he yearned to live and die.

The Deeds of Blessed Francis and His Companions
Ugolino Boniscambi of Montegiorgio

Chapter 6
The Lenten Fast of Saint Francis[30]

Because Francis, that very real servant of Christ, was in some things another Christ given to the world, God the Father made this fortunate man conformed in many things to Christ, his Son, as was apparent in his venerable band of holy companions, in the wonderful mystery of the stigmata of the Cross, and the holy fast of forty continuous days.

At one time when Francis was near the Lake of Perugia, he was at Mardi Gras a guest of a man devoted to him. He asked his host to take him for the love of God to an island on the lake where no one lived and to do so during the night before Ash Wednesday so that no one would know about it. The host did this very eagerly because of the great devotion he had for Francis. He prepared his little boat at night and transported him on Ash Wednesday to the island. Saint Francis brought nothing for food except two small loaves of bread.

After he reached the island he asked his ferryman to tell no one and to come back for him on Holy Thursday. Since there was no shelter there where he could rest, he crawled into a dense thicket where thorn bushes had

---

30. From *Early Documents: Volume 3 (The Prophet)*, 448.

formed an enclosure, and he stayed there immobile for the whole forty days, neither eating or drinking.

His host came looking for him, as they had agreed, on Holy Thursday and he found that, except for part of one, the two little loaves of bread had not been touched. It is believed that Saint Francis ate part of one loaf so that with a little bread he would expel the poison of vainglory and thus the glory of a forty day fast be reserved for the blessed Christ. Yet he did fast forty days and forty nights after the example of Christ.

In that place where Saint Francis did such remarkable penance, many miracles were performed through his merits. Therefore, people began to build and live on this island, and in a short period of time a large village and a house for the brothers were established there. The people of this village still show great reverence for that place where Saint Francis kept the Lenten fast.

Reflect or Discuss

1. What strikes you about the young Francis in the first story?

2. What does he do as a pilgrim in Rome that seems particularly youthful?

3. In the second account (or, in the similar one that appears in *The Little Flowers of Saint Francis* (*Early Documents: Vol. 3*, 578-79), it doesn't seem that Francis considered going to the island for Lenten practice in the company of others. What

do you think this reflects— his temperament, or his ascetic habits?

4. What does it say about Francis and food, during this fast?

5. Why would people begin to associate miracles with remarkable penance?

Reading 3

This text is from a later source called *The Conformity*, written about a century and a half after Francis's passing, and which glorifies both the person and the sanctity of the founder of the Franciscan way by highlighting the virtues of his life and how his life and way were imitations of the way and life of Christ.

This selection shows how meekness and humility—much praised by Jesus and exemplified in the earthly life of Jesus—were witnessed in Francis and in the lives of many of the early Franciscans.

The Conformity of the Life of Blessed Francis
to the Life of the Lord Jesus
Bartolomew of Pisa

Book Two

Francis abases himself[31]

The eleventh thing that manifests blessed Francis's humility is his meek life and manner. This was true of Christ, as he himself makes clear. At Mt 11:29 he says: "I am meek," that is, in manner, "and humble of heart." It is for this that Moses is commended, Nm 12:3, for "he was the most exceedingly meek of all the men who lived

---

31. *Early Documents, Vol. 4 (The Conformity), 2*; 224-27.

93

on earth." That blessed Francis had such a very humble and meek manner is proved by what we have said above and by many other facts: – First, because mild-natured animals loved to keep company with him. This is shown by the little lamb he was given in Rome; by the sheep that stayed in Saint Mary of the Angels; by the sheep who left their pasture and went to him when he was returning from Siena; by the little hare that kept leaping into his lap; by the baby rabbit that was given him on the Lake of Perugia. All these stories are related in Part VIII of the Legend. And because like consorts with like, Ecclus 14, the affection these timid animals had for him was an indication that he himself was very mild-natured. – Second, similar proof is offered by birds, who willingly approached him and stayed with him, as was shown when he climbed Mount La Verna. And what is even more astonishing, blessed Francis's meekness tamed fierce wild animals, as in the case of the ferocious wolf at Gubbio.... He made this wolf so tame that it lived and went about among the people like a lamb among sheep. – The third proof is affirmed by men. He converted three bloodthirsty robbers at Monte Casale and made them most humble, receiving them into the Order. – He did the same with a robber whose ferocity he changed to gentleness, and called him Brother Agnello. . . .

The twelfth and last of these proofs of blessed Francis's humility is his performance of the works of humility. This is abundantly clear from what has been said in this second part of this Conformity. . . . For he cared for lepers who were despised and wretched people, treating their ulcers, bandaging them, wiping away the pus and eagerly kissing their ulcerous sores. While in good health he himself always went out for bread. He served the brothers in order to show himself a General Minister both in name and in deed. He would sweep out churches and places, to show that he found humble duties pleasing. He resigned the office of General. Like the other brothers, he chose to have a guardian to obey until his death. He chose to live without a companion of his own, in order to demonstrate to everyone by his words, his conduct, his actions and his practice the perfection and humility upon which he had placed

the whole structure of his religion. It is clear from a consideration of all that has been said that blessed Francis, after the fashion of Our Lord Jesus Christ, was submissive to all, and abased by true humility, as the second part of this Conformity maintains.

Following the example of Francis the earliest brothers and his blessed companions wholly embraced holy humility, and possessed and held fast to her as the companion of holy poverty. Brother Masseo asked God to give him humility for a long time, and finally the Lord kindly granted this and gave it to him. . . . The same was true of Brother Bernard, Brother Giles, and Brother Juniper, and so too all the others who were renowned for this virtue. . . .

That the early brothers were grounded in humility, after the example of our blessed father, was illustrated by the example of a certain Master of Sacred Theology who was in the Order in the time of blessed Francis. This man was devoted to the Blessed Mary and had determined in his heart that whatever was asked of him for the love of the Virgin, if it were in his power, he would carry out at once. He revealed this intention of his to a certain noble lady, and she, seeing that he would be of use in, and was suited to the religious life, revealed his intention to some monks, persuading them to go to this master and ask him, for love of the Virgin, to become a monk, since because of his intention he would undoubtedly do so at once. The monks went to him and resolved to put this request to him at the end of their conversation, but after they had spoken with him at length, by God's will they forgot to mention the purpose of their visit.

When she learnt of this, the lady went to the Preachers and told them what she had said to the monks about the Master's intention and the petition they should make to him. The Friars Preacher went to him and as they discoursed at length with him on the virtues and comparative excellence of the Orders, a lay brother of our Order came along, an almoner of the Lesser Brothers, and asked for bread at the door of this Master. When no-one replied, he went up into the house to ask for bread as alms.

On seeing the Preachers conferring with this Master, he was suddenly prompted by the Holy Spirit and said to him: "I beg you, Master, for love of the Virgin Mary, Mother of God, to enter our Order." When he heard this the Master was utterly amazed, and he said to the lay brother: "Brother, go back to your house and have a habit ready: I shall gladly fulfill your request." And that is what happened. The Preachers, overcome with embarrassment, went back to their house without achieving their desire, while the Master became a devout and holy Lesser Brother.

Before this, the same Master had gone to Assisi out of reverence for blessed Francis, and lingered there and stayed so long that he was able to preach well in Italian. Blessed Clare was then alive, and when on one occasion she told the Guardian to send her one of the brothers to preach, the Guardian sent this Master to her monastery to preach. He had begun to speak and was preaching a magnificent sermon about God, when the holy Brother Giles, who was a lay brother and was then in that monastery and was listening to the sermon, suddenly rose up in utter fervor of spirit and said to the Master who was preaching: "Be silent, Master, because I want to speak for a moment." When the Master heard this he stopped preaching, covered his head with his hood, and humbly sat down. After Brother Giles had spoken as he wished, he said finally to the Master: "Up you get, brother. Finish your sermon." And he got up at once and finished the sermon he had begun.

When he had finished and left the place, blessed Clare said to the brothers who were present: "I tell you, brothers, today I have seen a marvel. Blessed Francis, my father and lord, once told me that he wanted his Order to show so much humility that if a Master of Theology were speaking, he would be silent at the bidding of even a lay person. This has today been fulfilled before my very eyes. And I tell you, brothers, that I have been more edified by that brother's humility than if I had seen him raise the dead."

We know of many other similar examples of humility in the other brothers, but let the above suffice. It was through humility that Brother Bernard of Quintavalle withdrew from Bologna, because he was receiving too much honor. And it was through humility that Rufino drove the devil from a man when he went begging for bread. And there are many other examples.

Reflect or Discuss

1. What does meekness have to do with being alone?

2. What does meekness have to do with solitude?

3. Is there a difference between being alone and solitude?

4. How might spending time alone with God help to develop the virtues of humility and meekness?

5. This is only the third time that Clare has appeared in our readings. What do you think of her comment about being more edified by the brother's actions than if she had seen him raise someone from the dead? Is she exaggerating?

Reading 4

Now, there are many descriptions in the early documents of Francis's encounter with Christ in a vision of a seraph upon Mount La Verna, but I like this one the best. It is a narrative, with wonderful, colorful context, and it does not focus on the stigmata wounds that Francis received that day, but rather, on other aspects of what occurred.

The Assisi Compilation

Chapter 118
He Has a Vision of the Winged Seraph During the Lent of
Saint Michael on La Verna[32]

One time blessed Francis went to the hermitage of Mount La Verna and because that place is very remote, he liked it very much, and he wanted to do a Lent in honor of Saint Michael. He went there before the feast of the Assumption of the glorious Virgin Mary, and he counted the days from the feast of Saint Mary to the feast of Saint Michael, which are forty days, and he said: "I want to make a Lent here, in honor of God, the Blessed Virgin Mary, His mother, and blessed Michael, the prince of angels and of souls."

And it happened as he entered his cell where he was to stay constantly, he asked the Lord on the first night to

---

32. *Early Documents, Vol. 2 (The Founder)*, 226-27.

show him in some way how he could know if it were His will for him to remain there.

When blessed Francis stayed constantly in a place to pray, or when he went through the world preaching, he was always anxious to know the will of the Lord, about how he could please Him better. He was sometimes afraid that, under the pretext of remaining in prayer in a remote place, the body wanted to rest, refusing the labor of going through the world preaching, for which Christ came down from heaven into this world. Indeed he would ask those he considered beloved by the Lord to ask Him to show them His will, whether he should go through the world preaching or stay for a while in a remote place to pray.

In early morning at dawn, while he stood in prayer, birds of various kinds came over the cell where he was staying. They did not come altogether, but first one would come and sing its sweet verse, and then go away, and another one come and sing and go away. They all did the same.

Blessed Francis was very happy at this and received great consolation from it. But when he began to meditate on what this might be, the Lord told him in spirit: "This is a sign that the Lord will do good for you in this cell and give you many consolations."

This was really true. Among all the consolations, hidden and manifest, which the Lord granted him, there was shown to him by the Lord a vision of a Seraph, from which, for the whole time of his life, he had great consolation in his soul between himself and the Lord. And it happened that while his companion brought him food that day, he told him everything that happened to him.

And, although he had many consolations in that cell, demons also gave him many trials at night, as he himself told his companion. That is why he once said: "If the brothers knew how many trials the demons cause me, there would not be one of them who would not have great piety and compassion for me."

As a result, as he often said to his companions, he was unable by himself to satisfy the brothers or sometimes to show them the friendliness which the brothers desired.

Reflect or Discuss

1. This is one of the examples of Francis observing multiples "Lents." Notice how he begins conversation with the Lord immediately upon arrival, about what many of us might consider small details.

2. In the early morning, what is his posture of prayer? Why might that have been the case?

3. What are the "consolations" that Francis receives? What is the meaning of a consolation in prayer?

4. In this scene—unlike some others that we've seen—Francis "tells all" to a companion who was with him upon the mountain. "He told him everything that happened," the text says. What are rea-

sons why we might share with a close friend what happens to us in prayer?

5. Why might we sometimes *not* want to share our prayer experiences?

Reading 5

In this reading, too, the details tell the story. This portion from Thomas of Celano's "Second Life" of Francis, known as *The Remembrance of the Desire of a Soul*, reveals how passionately Francis felt about the Portiuncula, the little chapel in the valley below Assisi, which was the mother house for all Franciscans of the first generation. It wasn't until after Francis's death, and the subsequently rapid construction of the great Basilica in his name in Assisi itself, that Saint Mary of the Portiuncula was replaced in this regard.

The Remembrance of the Desire of a Soul
Thomas of Celano

Chapter 12
Saint Mary of the Portiuncula—How the Saint Loved This
Place, How the Brothers Lived There, and How the Blessed
Virgin Loved It[33]

Francis, the servant of God,
was small in stature,
humble in attitude,
and lesser by profession.
While living in the world
he chose a little portion of the world
for himself and his followers,

---

33.   *Early Documents: Vol. 2 (The Founder)*, 256-58.

since he could not serve Christ
unless he had something of this world.
Since ancient times, prophetically,
this place was called "the Little Portion,"
since it was the lot ceded
to those who wished to hold nothing of this world.
In this place
there was a church built for the Virgin Mother,
who by her unique humility
deserved, after her Son, to be the head of all the saints.
It is here the Order of Lesser Ones
had its beginning.
As their numbers increased,
there "a noble structure arose
upon their solid foundation."
The saint loved this place more than any other.
He commanded his brothers
to venerate it with special reverence.
He wanted it, like a mirror of the Order,
always preserved in humility and highest poverty,
and therefore kept its ownership in the hands of others,
keeping for himself and his brothers only the use of it.

There the most rigid discipline was kept in all things:
as much in silence and in labor as in other religious obser-
vances. The entrance there was not open except to specially
selected brothers, gathered from every region, whom the
saint wanted to be truly devoted to God and perfect in
every respect. Similarly, entrance was completely forbidden to any secular person. He did not want the brothers
dwelling there—always kept below a certain number—to

have their ears itching for worldly news and, interrupting their contemplation of heavenly things, to be dragged down to dealing with lower things by the talk of gossips. No one was allowed to speak idle words there, nor to repeat those spoken by others. And, if anyone happened to do this, punishment taught him to avoid further harm and not to repeat this in the future. Day and night, without interruption, those living in the place were engaged in the praises of God and, scented with a wonderful fragrance, they led the life of angels. This was only right! According to the stories of the old neighbors, that church used to be called by another name, "Saint Mary of the Angels." As the blessed Father used to say, God revealed to him, that among all other churches built in her honor throughout the world, the blessed Virgin cherished that church with special affection. For that reason the saint also loved it more than all others.

Reflect or Discuss

>1. What does this selection from an early biography of Francis say about the connection he experienced between spending time with God and silence?

>2. There is natural silence (the absence of noise or disturbance), and then there is silence that is cultivated. What is the difference between the two? Do you value one more than the other?

>3. Why might it be necessary to turn away from the world in order to cultivate truly useful holy silence?

4. Can you think of praise for God that does not involve silence?

5. Can you recall instances in Francis's life when he praises the Lord noisily?

Reading 6

Lastly, this week, we read this memorable portion of the account of Francis's death from Thomas of Celano's "Second Life." We see that his death also offers examples of how someone on the Way of Saint Francis might treat silence and seek to spend time alone with God.

The Remembrance of the Desire of a Soul
Thomas of Celano

Chapter 163
His Death and What He Did Before It[34]

As the brothers shed bitter tears and wept inconsolably, the holy father had bread brought to him. He blessed and broke it, and gave each of them a piece to eat.

He also ordered a Book of the Gospels to be brought and asked that the Gospel according to Saint John be read to him starting from that place which begins: Before the feast of Passover. He was remembering that most sacred Supper, the last one the Lord celebrated with his disciples. In reverent memory of this, to show his brothers how much he loved them, he did all of this.

The few days that remained to him before his passing he spent in praise of God, teaching his beloved companions how to praise Christ with him. As best he could,

---

34. *Early Documents: Vol. 2 (The Founder)*, 387-88, corrected.

he broke out in this psalm, "With my voice I cried to the Lord, With my voice I beseeched the Lord." He also invited all creatures to the praise of God, and exhorted them to love by some words which he had composed earlier. Even death itself, terrible and hateful to everyone, he exhorted to praise, and going to meet her joyfully, invited her to be his guest, saying: "Welcome, my Sister Death!" And to the doctor he said: "Be bold, Brother Doctor, foretell death is near; for to me she will be the gate of Life!" But to the brothers he said: "When you see I have come to my end put me out naked on the ground as you saw me naked the day before yesterday, and once I am dead, allow me to lie there for as long as it takes to walk a leisurely mile."

The hour came.
All the mysteries of Christ
were fulfilled in him,
and he happily flew off to God.

Reflect or Discuss

1. Francis discerned early in his religious life that God didn't want him to become a contemplative monk. He was to be a friar instead. What are the differences between the two?

2. Francis praises God in these final scenes, but the implication of his praising is that it is noisy, not

quiet and subdued. How might time alone with God teach us to make noise?

3. What is Francis's final request of his friends?

4. How long does it take you to "walk a leisurely mile"?

5. Rabbi Nachman of Breslov used to say: "When someone is happy, it is easy for them to set aside time to express thoughts to God with a contrite heart, but when someone is depressed, it can be difficult to meditate or speak to God" (*Sichoth HaRan* 20). Do you agree? What does this suggest about the life of Francis and how he practiced praise and joy as well as tears and penance?

Week Three Prayer of Intention / Spiritual Practice

This would be a good place to offer suggestions for how you might rethink your life, this Lent, in order to find more periods of time alone, and in quiet, with God.

We all know how difficult it can be to do this.

We all know how much our screens divert us from these good intentions. It is almost as if our attention span has been permanently altered—shortened—by our devices. If you are like most people today, if you can spend even fifteen minutes a day in quiet with God, uninterrupted, you will be doing well.

So, ask yourself, now: How am I doing? What can I do better?

Consider some very ordinary factors, such as:

- Do I need a dedicated place or space to sit quietly with God uninterrupted?

- Do I need to leave my living space each day (go for a walk, etc.) in order to find the proper solitude?

- How might I impose Sabbath rules on the devices I use throughout the day, so as to not allow them to hijack the times I am setting aside to be alone with God?

You may want to make some notes right here in the book, to remind you of your holy intentions.

Week Four

Imitating Christ

This is where the lost art of compunction of Week Two—when we considered that a change of heart is what we hope for—seeks a fuller completion: penance, and the Christian life itself, is about becoming transformed. To imitate Christ is to seek to be more like him, in fact, to become more like him.

The language of this is nothing new. Before there was Thomas à Kempis, the fifteenth century author of the spiritual classic and bestseller, *The Imitation of Christ*, there was Francis of Assisi, whose biography demonstrates one of humanity's greatest attempts to imitate the life and teachings of Jesus.

Francis was so intent on imitating Jesus Christ in his actions and words that after Francis's death his followers became extreme in their claims to similarity between Francis and Jesus. They drew every imaginable parallel, as if Francis was a new Christ for all humankind. The stigmata extended this claim even further, as if the wounds of Christ in the flesh of Francis were somehow necessary to improve upon what Christ had done in his Incarnation and Passion. With good reason, there were some who then began to criticize these Franciscan interpretations, saying that they were confusing the saved with the savior.

Nevertheless, the plain truth is that this happened, in the first place, because Francis of Assisi was indeed intent on imitating his Lord down to the some of the smallest of details.

Why imitate the life of another, even the life of our Savior? The answer comes from our Savior himself:

> Jesus told his disciples, "If any want to become my followers, let them deny themselves and take up their cross and follow me." (Mt 16:24)

> So if I, your Lord and Teacher, have washed your feet, you also ought to wash one another's feet. For I have set you an example, that you also should do as I have done to you. (Jn 13:14-15)

St. Paul, too, wrote in his letters to early Christian communities:

> Therefore be imitators of God, as beloved children, and live in love, as Christ loved us and gave himself up for us, a fragrant offering and sacrifice to God. (Eph 5:1-2)

> And it is no longer I who live, but it is Christ who lives in me. And the life I now live in the flesh I live by faith in the Son of God, who loved me and gave himself for me. (Gal 2:20)

Paul also repeatedly praised people of faith in communities for which he was spiritually responsible (in Corinth, in Rome, etc.) for imitating him, because by imitating him they were also imitating Christ. "Be imitators of me, as I am of Christ" (1 Cor. 11:1), Paul said.

For these reasons, imitating Jesus Christ has been the central path of Christian formation since the time of the early church. This is the ultimate purpose of penance and Lent as a way of life.

Reading 1

This reading is interesting in how it summarizes the spiritual practices of Francis and the first men and women who followed him on the Franciscan way. They seem to have embodied the teachings of the Gospel, including some of the teachings that are uncomfortable to follow to the letter, and by doing so their witness even prompted people of worldly power to a life of penance.

A Book of the Praises of Saint Francis
Bernard of Besse

From *Chapter 2*
The Formation of the First Disciples[35]

Since they looked down on all earthly things and never loved themselves selfishly, they poured out all their loving affection in common, hiring themselves out to provide for the others' need, seeking not their own interests but those of Christ and of their neighbors.

Once when a simpleton was throwing stones at the brothers, one brother placed himself in front of them, rejoicing that he would be struck rather than his companion.

Rooted in charity and humility, one respected the other as if he were his master. Whoever among them

---

35. *Early Documents: Vol. 3 (The Prophet)*, 39.

excelled because of a position or grace seemed even more humble and self-effacing than the others. If anyone happened to say something that displeased another, he would not rest until, with the greatest humility, he confessed his fault to that brother. They gathered together out of desire, and were delighted to stay together; but they found separation hard, parting bitter. But truly obedient soldiers, they never dared to place anything before holy obedience, knowing nothing about distinguishing precepts. They almost ran headlong, to carry out what they were asked with no thought of contradicting it.

Whatever they were ordered, they considered to be the Lord's will. Thus it was pleasant and easy for them to fulfill everything. They eagerly asked not to be sent to the lands of their origin so that they might observe the words of the Prophet: I have become an outcast to my brothers, a stranger to my mother's sons.

They always found themselves in the Spirit's joy, because they did not possess the stuff of turmoil. They exulted in tribulations as those placed at a great advantage, and they prayed to God for their persecutors. Seeing this, many were converted to them.

When the rich of the world went out of their way to visit them, they received them quickly and kindly, and would invite them to call them back from evil, and prompt them to penance. Wherever they met men on the roads or in the piazzas, the brothers would encourage them to love and to fear their Creator. They would more willingly accept hospitality among priests than among other seculars. But when they could not obtain lodging, they would inquire who in that place was God-fearing with whom they could be more suitably lodged. And although they were extremely poor, they were always generous in giving to all who asked of them, sharing the alms given to them.

Reflect or Discuss

1. Compare this passage from Bernard of Besse to the Beatitudes of Jesus (Mt. 5:1-11).

When Jesus saw the crowds, he went up the mountain; and after he sat down, his disciples came to him. Then he began to speak, and taught them, saying:

"Blessed are the poor in spirit, for theirs is the kingdom of heaven.

"Blessed are those who mourn, for they will be comforted.

"Blessed are the meek, for they will inherit the earth.

"Blessed are those who hunger and thirst for righteousness, for they will be filled.

"Blessed are the merciful, for they will receive mercy.

"Blessed are the pure in heart, for they will see God.

"Blessed are the peacemakers, for they will be called children of God.

"Blessed are those who are persecuted for righteousness' sake, for theirs is the kingdom of heaven.

"Blessed are you when people revile you and persecute you and utter all kinds of evil against you falsely on my account. Rejoice and be glad, for your reward is great in heaven, for in the same way they persecuted the prophets who were before you."

2. Which of the Beatitudes seems perhaps "too good to be true"?

3. Do these actions of Francis and the early friars sound like Christian practice today?

4. Why do you think we've stopped doing some of these things, today?

5. Look again at the fifth paragraph and that phrase, "the Spirit's joy." What might that mean?

Reading 2

There's no question that Francis modeled his life, even down to many of its most minute details, after the life of Christ as we discover it in the gospels. As we've noted, sometimes in the early texts these comparisons seem to have gone too far—but what follows is a summary that seems accurate and reasonable.

The Conformity of the Life of Blessed Francis to the Life of the Lord Jesus
Bartolomew of Pisa

Second Prologue, I[36]

The devout Brother Bonaventure expresses . . . perfectly when he says of blessed Francis in Part IX of his *Major Legend*: "Who would be competent to describe the burning charity with which Francis, the friend of the Bridegroom, was aflame? Like a burning coal, he seemed totally absorbed in the flame of divine love. For as soon as he heard mention of 'the love of the Lord' he was excited, moved, and on fire as if these words from the outside were a plectrum strumming the strings of his heart on the inside." He also said many other things on the subject. Though it is clear from what we have said that blessed Francis loved God and cleaved to him alone,

---

36.   *Early Documents (The Conformity) IV/1,* 70-72.

it can be demonstrated by many other proofs as well. Many things show that he cleaved totally to Christ the Lord and placed all his confidence in him.

First, his loving and caring for the poor and outcast, viz. the lepers, by serving them, helping them and doing them kindnesses; this was shown in the case of the naked soldier whom blessed Francis clothed; in the case of the leper, to whom he gave money, and kissed; and similarly in many other cases.

Second, his abandoning the world for Christ, when he renounced his father and all claims on his father's possessions before the bishop.

Third, he was visited by an apparition of one Crucified, who seemed to Francis as it were fixed to a cross, and so pierced his soul with the intensity of his Passion that thereafter, whenever he recalled this, he could scarcely keep himself from weeping and groaning, and the memory of this Passion was always present before the eyes of his soul.

Fourth, his joyful acceptance of every sort of disgrace for Christ. He was pelted by his fellow citizens with the mud of the streets and with stones, was subjected to beating by his father, and laughed at by his brother; and finally he went begging, and casting shame aside, bore all this with joy.

Fifth, his restoration of the church of San Damiano in accordance with the command of the Crucified, which he had first wanted to do by selling many of his own effects; but at length he restored that church to the state it is in today, together with two others.

Sixth, his adoption of the Gospel life in everything. Francis observed the holy Gospel to the letter, not transgressing one jot or tittle of it. And only he and his friars have a Rule that, in its special tone and form, is founded on the Gospel.

Seventh, the help given him by Christ. For Christ helped him in everything. It was clear at the confirmation of his Rule when He moved his Vicar by a vision to give the servant of God a kindly hearing and yield to his requests; when he helped Francis as he was leaving Rome with his companions after the confirmation of the Rule; and, when alms were given him by God over many days on the Sea of Slavonia, and he nourished all who were with him at sea; also when at the General Chapter at Saint Mary of the Portiuncula, where there were more than 5,000 brothers, he furnished all the necessary provisions in ample sufficiency.

Eighth, his love, embrace and betrothal of poverty for love of Christ. This he loved more than anything, and in it he tried to surpass all others. . . .

Ninth, his meditation upon, preaching of, glorying in and contemplation of the Crucified. He neither preached, nor understood, nor contemplated anything else, and he repeatedly told the brothers that there was nothing they need constantly meditate and reflect upon other than the Lord's Passion, as was demonstrated and proved by abundant evidence. The fact that he constantly meditated upon the cross was revealed to Brother Leo, who saw the crucified Christ go before blessed Francis in a great blaze of light, when he was going once to Saint

Mary of the Angels. That he preached the Crucified was proved when Brother Pacifico saw him, while preaching, "marked with two brightly shining swords intersecting in the shape of a cross." That he contemplated the cross in his prayer was clear from his being lifted in the air in the shape of a cross. And that he gloried in, and studied nothing else was clear from the reply he made to one of his companions; for when blessed Francis was gravely ill and warned by a certain brother that he should have something read to him, he retorted that he needed nothing more, because, he said, "I know Jesus," the poor "crucified one."

Tenth, the many times he was visited by Christ. Oh, how many times the Lord Jesus Christ himself deigned to appear to blessed Francis! And he was visited not only by Christ himself, but by the Blessed Virgin, John the Baptist, John the Evangelist, the holy Apostles Peter and Paul, the Archangel Michael and the holy Angels, as will be clear in the appropriate contexts below. But I shall touch on just two occasions when the child Christ Jesus appeared miraculously to him: the first was when blessed Francis recreated at Greccio the scene of the Nativity, and held Christ in his arms and cradled him, as was witnessed by the knight John of Greccio; the second was when he was praying to the Virgin that she might grant him some consolation concerning the tiny Jesus, and the most beautiful Virgin herself stood by him and held out Jesus in her arms to blessed Francis, and gave him to him to hold and kiss from nightfall until daybreak.

Eleventh, Francis's overcoming of the devil; by the power of the good Jesus he conquered the devil in the hermitage at Sarteano, vanquished him at night in churches, and expelled him from the city of Arezzo and from many other cities, as will be told below.

Twelfth, his demonstration of his wholehearted desire to die for Christ. For he went three times to the territory of the Saracens hoping to win the palm of martyrdom for Christ, but failed to achieve what he desired because God was preserving him for the faithful.

Reflect or Discuss

1. It is natural for us to try and "read between the lines" in accounts of Francis's life and doings, such as these. For example, what does an account such as this *not include*? For example, was Francis ever depressed? Was he ever without hope? Did he feel, at times, abandoned by God?

2. What do you think is the best definition of a saint?

3. Does a text such as this indicate how and why Francis is a saint? How does it? How does it not?

4. Does every Christian have a saintly vocation?

5. Are there specific ways in your life that someone might say—to adopt a phrase from the first paragraph above—that you "cleaved to Christ the Lord and placed your confidence in him"?

Reading 3

To read some of the early texts, you might come to believe that Francis never did wrong, never sinned. But of course he did sin and he freely admitted so on many occasions. In order to keep any discussion of imitating Christ in proper perspective, we will highlight one of these ways here.

The framing of these scenes as conversations between Francis and the devil are a narrative structure of Celano that, in itself, reveals how we've long associated Francis with imitating Christ. You may want to re-familiarize yourself with the scene of Jesus being tempted by the devil as relayed in the Gospel of Matthew 4:1-11.

This account should be read in connection with those presented as Reading 3 of Week One ("Lent as a Balanced Way of Life"), when Francis insisted on public confession for his own private sins.

In part thanks to G. K. Chesterton's little book about St. Francis, this is one of the most iconic and colorful scenes from Francis's life . . .

The Remembrance of the Desire of a Soul
Thomas of Celano

The Second Book

Chapter 82

*How the Devil Called Him and Tempted Him to Lust and
How the Saint Overcame It*[37]

In the brothers' hermitage at Sarteano that evil
one who always envies the progress of God's children
dared to attempt something against the saint. Seeing
that the holy man was becoming even holier, and not
overlooking today's profit because of yesterday's, as the
saint gave himself one night to prayer in his cell, the evil
one called him three times: "Francis! Francis! Francis!"
And he replied saying: "What do you want?" The reply
was: "There is no sinner in the world whom the Lord
will not forgive if he is converted. But if anyone kills
himself by hard penance, for all eternity he will find no
mercy." At once by a revelation, the saint recognized the
enemy's cunning, how he was trying to call him back to
being lukewarm. What then? The enemy did not give
up. He tried a new line of attack. Seeing that he had
not been able to hide this snare, he prepared a different
one, namely, an urge of the flesh. But to no use, since the
one who detected a clever trick of the spirit could not
be fooled by the flesh. The devil sent into him a violent
temptation to lust, but as soon as the blessed father felt
it, he took off his clothes and lashed himself furiously
with the cord, saying: "Come on, Brother Ass, that's the
way you should stay under the whip! The tunic belongs to
religion: no stealing allowed! If you want to leave, leave!"

However, when he saw that the temptation did not
leave even after the discipline, though he painted welts

37. *Early Documents, Vol. 2 (The Founder)*, 324-25.

all over his limbs black and blue, he opened the cell, went out to the garden, and threw himself naked into the deep snow. Taking snow by the handful he packed it together into balls and made seven piles. Showing them to himself, he began to address his body: "Here, this large one is your wife, and those four over there are your two sons and your two daughters; the other two are your servant and your maid who are needed to serve them. So hurry," he said, "get all of them some clothes, because they're freezing to death! But if complicated care of them is annoying, then take care to serve one Master!" At that the devil went away in confusion, and the saint returned to his cell praising God. A certain spiritual brother was giving himself to prayer at that time, and he saw it all in the bright moonlight. When the saint later learned that the brother had seen him that night, he was very disturbed, and ordered him not to reveal it to anyone as long as he lived in the world.

Reflect or Discuss

1. How does this anecdote reflect a similarity to the life of Christ? Which details seem familiar?

2. Look at how the word "flesh" is used here. What might "flesh" mean, in a broader sense? What other words come to mind?

3. What do you make of the conversation he has with the devil?

4. How does this suggest an example of how we might imitate Christ even when we are tempted to sin?

5. Although we may not actually have conversations with the devil, how do we perhaps still encounter him in other places and in other ways?

Reading 4

Jesus's example and teaching to share the Good News, love one's neighbor, love one's enemy, are all exemplified in a variety of anecdotes from Francis's life. But perhaps none of them is more emblematic of Francis's conversion than his visit to the Sultan during the Crusades. This is how Thomas of Celano tells the story. (Bonaventure added many details and other layers to the story, in his later account.)

The Life of Saint Francis
Thomas of Celano

Chapter 20
The Desire to Undergo Martyrdom Which Took Him
First to Spain and Then Journeying to Syria;
And How God Saved Sailors from Danger,
Multiplying Their Supply of Food[38]

Burning with divine love,
the blessed father Francis was always eager to try
his hand at brave deeds,
and walking in the way of God's commands
with heart wide-open,
he longed to reach the summit of perfection.

38.　*Early Documents: Vol. 1 (The Saint)*, 229-31.

In the sixth year of his conversion, burning with the desire for holy martyrdom, he wished to take a ship to the region of Syria to preach the Christian faith and repentance to the Saracens and other unbelievers. But after he had boarded a ship to go there, contrary winds started blowing, and he found himself with his fellow travelers on the shores of Slavonia.

When he realized that he had been cheated of what he desired, after a little while he begged some sailors going to Ancona to take him with them, since there were hardly any ships that could sail that year to Syria. But the sailors stubbornly refused to do so since he could not pay them. The holy one of God, trusting God's goodness, secretly boarded the ship with his companion. By divine providence, a man arrived unknown to anyone, who brought the food needed. He called over a person from the ship, a God-fearing man. "Take with you all these things," he said, "and in their time of need faithfully give them to those poor men hiding on your ship."

A great storm arose and they had to spend many days laboring at the oars. They had used up all their food. Only the food of the poor Francis remained. Owing to divine grace and power, his food multiplied so much that, although there were still many days of sailing remaining, it fully supplied the needs of them all until they reached the port of Ancona. When the sailors realized that they had escaped the dangers of the sea through God's servant Francis, they gave thanks to almighty God, who is always revealed through his servants as awesome and loving.

Francis, the servant of the most high, left the sea and began to walk the earth. Furrowing with the plough of the word, he sowed the seed of life, bearing blessed fruit. Soon many good and suitable men, cleric and lay, fleeing the world and courageously escaping the devil, by the grace and will of the Most High, followed him devoutly in his life and proposal.

Though the shoot of the gospel was producing choice fruit in abundance, it did not stifle his highest purpose, the burning desire for martyrdom. Not too long after this, he began to travel towards Morocco to preach the gospel of Christ. . . . He was so carried away with desire that he would sometimes leave behind his companion on the journey and hurry ahead, intoxicated in spirit, in order to carry out his purpose. But the good God, out of pure kindness, was pleased to be mindful of me and many others. After he reached Spain God withstood him to his face, striking him with illness, and called him back from the journey he had begun.

Shortly afterwards when Francis returned to the Church of Saint Mary of the Portiuncula, some literate men and nobles gladly joined him. He received such men with honor and dignity, since he himself was very noble and distinguished in spirit, and respectfully gave to each his due. In fact, since he was endowed with outstanding discernment, he wisely considered in all matters the dignity of rank of each one.

But still he would not rest from carrying out fervently the holy impulse of his spirit. Now in the thirteenth year of his conversion, he journeyed to the region of Syria, while bitter and long battles were being waged daily between Christians and pagans. Taking a companion with him, he was not afraid to present himself to the sight of the Sultan of the Saracens.

Who is equal to the task of telling this story?

What great firmness he showed standing in front of him!

With great strength of soul he spoke to him, with eloquence and confidence he answered those who insulted the Christian law.

Before he reached the Sultan, he was captured by soldiers, insulted and beaten, but was not afraid. He did not flinch at threats of torture nor was he shaken by death threats. Although he was ill-treated by many with a hostile spirit and a harsh attitude, he was received very graciously by the Sultan. The Sultan honored him as much as he could, offering him many gifts, trying to turn his mind to worldly riches. But when he saw that he resolutely scorned all these things like dung, the Sultan was overflowing with admiration and recognized him as a man unlike any other. He was moved by his words and listened to him very willingly.

> In all this, however,
> the Lord did not fulfill his desire,
> reserving for him the prerogative of a unique grace.

Reflect or Discuss

1. Those of us walking the Franciscan Way sometimes forget that we are meant to be preachers, or at least, evangelists and missioners. What does this

iconic scene from Francis's life say about Francis as a preacher and missioner?

2. What did martyrdom have to do with evangelization in Francis's era? What sort of "martyrdom" do we potentially face for our evangelization efforts in our much more comfortable situations in the twenty-first century west?

3. What does martyrdom have to do with imitating Christ?

4. Notice the contrast between Francis's treatment at the hands of Christian soldiers and his treatment by the Sultan and his men.

5. What does Francis's visit to the Sultan have to do with imitating Christ?

Reading 5

In two short selections, here, we see Francis appealing to the teachings of Christ for ultimate guidance. First, from the writings of Francis himself, we have a portion from his *Rule* in which he outlines the first essential presupposition for becoming a Franciscan.

The Later Rule (1223)

Francis of Assisi

From *Chapter 2*
*Those Who Wish to Adopt This Life, and How They
Should Be Received*[39]

If there are any who wish to accept this life and come to our brothers, let them send them to their provincial ministers, to whom alone and not to others is permission granted to receive the brothers. Let the ministers examine them carefully concerning the Catholic faith and the sacraments of the Church. If they believe all these things, will faithfully profess them, and steadfastly observe them to the end; and if they have no wives, or if they have wives who have already taken a vow of continence and are of such an age that suspicion cannot be raised about them, and who have already entered a monastery or have

---

39. *Early Documents, Vol. 1 (The Saint)*, 100.

given their husbands permission by the authority of the bishop of the diocese, let the ministers speak to them the words of the holy Gospel that they go and sell all they have and take care to give it to the poor. If they cannot do this, their good will may suffice. Let the brothers and the minister be careful not to interfere with their temporal goods that they may dispose of their belongings as the Lord inspires them. If, however, counsel is sought, the minister may send them to some God-fearing persons according to whose advice their goods may be distributed to the poor.

Second, look again at what is perhaps a familiar story to you—the conversion of the first two men to follow Francis in his way of life, and how together all three of them determined the course of their penance and spiritual practice. There are many accounts of this episode; this one is my favorite because of all the rich surrounding details demonstrating how attentive Francis was to imitating his Lord.

The Legend of Three Companions

Chapter 8
Hearing and Understanding the Counsels of Christ in the Gospel, He Immediately Changed His External Garb and Put on a New Habit of Internal and External Perfection[40]

---

40.   *Early Documents, Vol. 2 (The Founder)*, 84-86.

While he was completing the church of San Damiano, blessed Francis wore the habit of a hermit: a staff in his hand, shoes on his feet, and a leather belt around his waist.

Then, one day at Mass, he heard those things which Christ tells the disciples who were sent out to preach, instructing them to carry no gold or silver, a wallet or a purse, bread, walking stick, or shoes, or two tunics. After understanding this more clearly because of the priest, he was filled with indescribable joy. "This," he said, "is what I want to do with all my strength."

And so, after committing to memory everything he had heard, he joyfully fulfilled them, removed his second garment without delay, and from then on never used a walking stick, shoes, purse, or wallet. He made for himself a very cheap and plain tunic, and, throwing the belt away, he girded himself with a cord.

Applying all the care of his heart to observe the words of new grace as much as possible, he began, inspired by God, to be a messenger of evangelical perfection and, in simple words, to preach penance in public. His words were neither hollow nor ridiculous, but filled with the power of the Holy Spirit, penetrating the marrow of the heart, so that listeners were turned to great amazement.

As he later testified, he learned a greeting of this sort by the Lord's revelation: "May the Lord give you peace!" Therefore, in all his preaching, he greeted the people at the beginning of his sermon with a proclamation of peace.

It is certainly astonishing, if not miraculous, that this greeting of peace was used before his conversion by a precursor who frequently went through Assisi greeting the people with "Peace and good! Peace and good!" It seems plausible that, as John heralded Christ but withdrew when Christ began his mission of preaching, so too, like another John, this man preceded Francis in using the greeting of peace, but disappeared when he appeared.

Immediately, therefore, filled with the spirit of the prophets, the man of God, Francis, after that greeting, proclaimed peace, preached salvation, and, according to a prophetic passage, by his salutary admonitions, brought to true peace many who had previously lived at odds with Christ and far from salvation.

As both the truth of blessed Francis's simple teaching as well as that of his life became known to many, two years after his conversion, some men began to be moved to do penance by his example and, leaving all things, they joined him in life and habit. The first of these was Brother Bernard of holy memory.

He knew well how luxuriously blessed Francis had lived in the world; now he observed his constancy and zeal in the divine service, how, in particular, he was restoring dilapidated churches with a great deal of work, and what an austere life he was leading. He planned wholeheartedly to give everything he possessed to the poor, and, with determination, to join him in life and garb.

Therefore, one day approaching the man of God in secret, he disclosed his plan to him, and arranged to have him come that evening to his home. Thanking God, for he did not then have a companion, blessed Francis was overjoyed, especially since Lord Bernard was a person of great stature.

On the appointed evening, blessed Francis came to his house, his heart filled with great joy, and spent that whole night with him. Among many things, Lord Bernard said to him: "If, for many years, someone holds on to the possessions, many or few, he has acquired from his lord, and no longer wishes to keep them, what is the better thing for him to do with them?" Blessed Francis answered that he must give back to the lord what was received from him. And Lord Bernard said: "Then, brother, I want to give away all my worldly goods for the love of my Lord who gave them to me, as it seems best to you." The saint told him: "We will go to the church early in the morning and, through the book of the Gospels, we will learn how the Lord instructed his disciples."

Rising at daybreak, then, together with another man named Peter, who also wanted to become a brother, they went to the church of San Nicolò next to the piazza of the city of Assisi. They entered for prayer, but, because they were simple, they did not know how to find the passage in the Gospel about renunciation. They prayed devoutly that the Lord would show them his will on opening the book the first time.

Once they had finished prayer, blessed Francis took the closed book and, kneeling before the altar, opened it. At its first opening, the Lord's counsel confronted them: *If you wish to be perfect, go, sell everything you possess and give to the poor, and you will have a treasure in heaven.*

Blessed Francis was overjoyed when he read this passage and thanked God. But since he was a true worshiper of the Trinity, he desired it to be confirmed by a threefold affirmation. He opened the book a second and a third time. When he opened it up the second time he saw: Take nothing for your journey, etc., and at the third opening: If any man wishes to come after me, he must deny himself, etc.

Each time he opened the book, blessed Francis thanked God for confirming his plan and the desire he had conceived earlier. After the third divine confirmation was pointed out and explained, he said to those men, Bernard and Peter: "Brothers, this is our life and rule and that of all who will want to join our company. Go, therefore, and fulfill what you have heard."

Then Lord Bernard, who was very rich, after selling all he had and acquiring a large sum of money, went and distributed it all to the city's poor. Peter likewise followed the divine counsel according to his means.

After getting rid of everything, they both received the habit which the saint had adopted after he put aside the habit of a hermit; and, from that hour, they lived with him according to the form of the holy Gospel as the Lord had shown them. This is why blessed Francis said in his Testament: "The Lord Himself revealed to me that I should live according to the form of the holy Gospel."

Reflect or Discuss

1. How does one become a friar minor, according to the instruction of Francis in the *Rule*? Notice how, after the basics are covered, Francis transitions to, "let the ministers speak to them the words of the holy Gospel. . ." What follows, then, is Matthew 19:21: "Jesus said to him, 'If you wish to be perfect, go, sell your possessions, and give the money to the poor, and you will have treasure in heaven; then come, follow me.'"

2. In the narrative from *The Legend of Three Companions* there are two more counsels from the Gospels that the brothers read together. Find a Bible and read these in their context.

"Take nothing for your journey. . ." is Luke 9:3.

"If any man wishes to come after me. . ." is Matthew 16:24.

3. Interesting detail: Notice that there is no priest there with the men, opening the book of Gospels. (There is not, in Bonaventure's later, "authoritative" account, either.) This is why it concludes with that final sentence. Read that final sentence again, and ponder: Does it matter that the men did this discernment on their own?

4. What does "The Lord Himself revealed to me. . ." mean?

5. Does the Lord reveal to you?

Reading 6

Poverty, humility, and obedience were the containers for Francis's imitation of Christ. Those three vows were not and are not special to Franciscans—they are shared by many who take vows in religious orders. Still, we see Francis molding himself in those three vows in special ways that imitate the Jesus of the gospels.

Any Christian today can do likewise, even amid a "secular" life. Poverty might equal detachment from possessions and also giving away what we don't need. Humility might equal a willingness to be corrected and to listen; also, a reluctance to assume authority. And obedience might equal readiness and courage to live counter-culturally in the world, to be willing, even, to be called a "fool" for living in ways of faithfulness to the teachings of Jesus.

For this final reading, we see two examples of the very active faith and love of Francis for Christ, in Christ, as Christ in the world. How did he maintain such an active approach? These two texts may point us in concrete directions.

Earlier Exhortation
To the Brothers and Sisters of Penance
(The First Version of the Letter to the Faithful)

Francis of Assisi

From *Chapter 1: Those Who Do Penance*[41]

---

41.   *Early Documents, Vol. 1 (The Saint)*, 41-42.

All those who love the Lord with their whole heart, with their whole soul and mind, with their whole strength and love their neighbors as themselves, who hate their bodies with their vices and sins, who receive the Body and Blood of our Lord Jesus Christ, and who produce worthy fruits of penance. O how happy and blessed are these men and women while they do such things and persevere in doing them, because the Spirit of the Lord will rest upon them and make Its home and dwelling place among them, and they are children of the heavenly Father Whose works they do, and they are spouses, brothers, and mothers of our Lord Jesus Christ.

We are spouses when the faithful soul is joined by the Holy Spirit to our Lord Jesus Christ. We are brothers to Him when we do the will of the Father who is in heaven. We are mothers when we carry Him in our heart and body through a divine love and a pure and sincere conscience and give birth to Him through a holy activity which must shine as an example before others.

The Major Legend of Saint Francis

Bonaventure of Bagnoregio

From the *Prologue*[42]

The grace of God our Savior has appeared
in these last days
in his servant Francis

---

42.   *Early Documents, Vol. 2 (The Founder)*, 525-26.

to all who are truly humble and lovers of holy poverty,
who, while venerating in him God's superabundant
mercy,
learn by his example
to reject wholeheartedly ungodliness and worldly
passions,
to live in conformity with Christ
and to thirst after blessed hope with unflagging desire.

In an outpouring of kindness,
the Most High God looked upon him,
a little, poor, and contrite man,
so that He not only lifted the needy man
from the dust of a worldly life;
but also gave him as a light for believers,
a practitioner, a leader, and a herald of Gospel perfection,
that by bearing witness to the light
he might prepare for the Lord a way of light and peace
to the hearts of his faithful.

Reflect or Discuss

1. Read the first sentence of the first selection again.
Our theme these four weeks has been penance and
the Lenten life. What does that first sentence say
about penance?

2. When, in the words of Francis, are we "spouses,"
"brothers," and "mothers"?

3. In the second selection, Bonaventure says that the grace of God appears to all who "reject wholeheartedly ungodliness and worldly passions." What might that look like?

4. Bonaventure says that the grace of God appears to all who "live in conformity with Christ." In your life, what does that look like?

5. Finally, the grace of God appears to all who "thirst after blessed hope with unflagging desire." What would it look like if people on the Franciscan Way did this today?

Week Four Prayer of Intention / Spiritual Practice

We could do no better to conclude Week Four, and this entire devotional study, than prepare ourselves to be more zealous and passionate. We have good ideas; we know what we ought to do; we are committed. Now we need the energy and zest and spiritedness to do this good work each day.

Here are a few spiritual-physical exercises you might try.

1) Sing in the morning, even if you aren't a singer. Or shout, if you'd rather not sing. These are physical exercises that nearly everyone can do and will give you a sense of waking your soul for the day ahead. You might start with the hymn, "Jesus, My Lord, My God, My All" (you'll find it in a few versions easily on YouTube; I like The Singing Nuns!). Or simply wake up and shout, "Come Holy Ghost"!

2) Carry reminders in your pockets. Some people carry rosaries. Others carry holy medals. I have friends who have prayer cards and saint cards in their wallets. If a rosary or a medal or some other object in your pocket will remind you of your penance, then carry it. If you are more of a word-focused person, look back through this book and find the phrases and short teachings that will remind you of what you need to do and write those down on a small card; carry the card with you. This then becomes as

Week Four

important to be on your person as your credit cards and keys, or even more so.

3) Do penance through prayer. This seems almost too simple to mention, but ask God for help. Ask often. Ask God to act in you. Tell God that you are ready and willing to change for him. As Francis of Assisi himself said:

[H]ow happy and blessed are those who love God and do as the Lord Himself says in the Gospel: "You shall love the Lord your God with all your heart and all your mind, and your neighbor as yourself." Let us love God, therefore, and adore Him with a pure heart and a pure mind. . . . And day and night let us direct praises and prayers to Him, saying: "Our Father, Who art in heaven". . .for we should pray always and not become weary.

From the "Later Admonition and Exhortation To the Brothers and Sisters of Penance (Second Version of the Letter to the Faithful)[43]

---

43. *Early Documents: Vol. 1 (The Saint)*, 46-47.

144